Poetic Reflections
At The Creekside

To BILL AND
DOROTHY
Clark Crouch

i

Publications by The Resource Network

Western Poetry Publications Imprint
Where Horses Reign, 2004
Sun, Sand & Soapweed, 2005
Western Images, 2007
Eight Viewpoints, 2009
Views from the Saddle, 2009
Harkin' Home, 2010
Thirty: poems from The Country Register, 2013
Rustic Ruminations, 2013
Prairie Knights (in press)
Western Poetry Anthology (in press)

Creekside Poetry Publications Imprint
Poetic Reflections At The Creekside, 2013

Two earlier books, *Voices of the Wind* and *Reflections,* were published by iUniverse.
All publications are available internationally through local and internet booksellers.

Poetic Reflections
At The Creekside

a poetic anthology by

Poets of the Great Northwest
*Poets*West @ The Creekside

and

Residents of The Creekside
A Merrill Gardens Retirement Community

Edited by Clark Crouch
Cover Photo by Laura Shreck

Creekside Poetry Publications
[An imprint of The Resource Network}
Woodinville, Washington

Poetic Reflections
At The Creekside

Information and Permissions
Creekside Poetry Publications
18200 Wood-Sno Rd NE
Woodinville, WA 98072

ISBN-13: 978-1494404123
ISBN-10: 1494404125

10 9 8 7 6 5 4 3 2

Preface

This is an eclectic collection...in effect, a virtual open mic in printed form...featuring poetry authored by Northwest poets who have performed at The Creekside as well as poetry by residents of The Creekside. The poems have been collected and accepted with regard for substance – poems such as one might hear and appreciate at a traditional open mic performance.

The Creekside is a Merrill Gardens Retirement Community where visiting Northwestern poets offer contemporary literary enlightenment for the entertainment of the residents and the community at large. In addition, the poets themselves enjoy the opportunity to share their work with a real and appreciative audience. These poets are extremely talented, dedicated, and exceptional in their approach to poetic expression and we value their contribution to the poetic genre.

Early decisions were made to avoid the restriction of a pervading theme and to permit any style of poetry whether in modern, traditional, or poetic prose forms. Thus, the poetic topics and reflections differ significantly but, collectively, they capture a magnificent view of facets of life in the Northwest and, yes, even of the nation and the world.

We greatly appreciate the support provided by *Poets*West, a Seattle based nonprofit organization which associated with The Creekside poetic venue in 2011 and which has facilitated the appearance of outstanding poets to be featured at monthly meetings of *Poets*West @ The Creekside.

Finally, we appreciate the photographic talents of Laura Shreck (1986-2013) whose work appears on the cover of this book as well as on four other books published by The Resource Network over the past several years. A very talented young woman…photographer, watercolorist, and missionary…who just recently lost a battle with cancer.

Clark Crouch, Editor
Creekside Poetry Publications
Woodinville, Washington

December 2013

"Painting is poetry that is seen rather than felt, and poetry is painting that is felt rather than seen." — *Leonardo da Vinci*

Contents by Author

Poems by Title

The Lady in Blue

~~ Peggy Barnett – ©2012 ~~

Yesterday I framed my Fra Angelico prints of angels .
I had bought them many years ago in Florence.
Set into a long gold frame with
four little squares edged in gold rope
the winged musician angels float in a gold sky
harps, violas, trumpets held high.

The lady in the blue dress is beautiful.
Her robe
the blue of the deepest blue sky day,
swirls around her feet.
Covering her golden hair is a blue gauze veil,
her blue eyes gaze upward,
her eyebrows a pencil thin line,
barely there.
A tiny red mouth between pale peach cheeks
in an oval face tilted slightly to the right.
She floats on a cloud,
sun rays streaming from behind her gold haloed head.
Golden stars surround her.
She holds a little golden haired child
that gazes at me.
A gilded frame of lilies in green leaves
winds around the edge of the card,
the size of a playing card,
given to me by Soeur Ann Marie,
the nun who is my teacher.

It is a painting of the Virgin Mary
but I don't know that.
I am the little five year old
Jewish girl in the jungle
with no other school to go to

than the local Catholic Convent school.
My sister takes me every morning
on the back of her bicycle.
When it rains
great big drops one by one spaced far apart
turn the road to mud
so we walk instead.
I love the picture of the Lady in Blue.
She is so beautiful.
But my mother takes it away
after she finds out that I have been to confession
on my knees at the altar
had opened my lips for the wafer-of-no-taste
to melt on my tongue
had sipped sweet wine from the small silver chalice.
After that I sit in the back of the church
the outcast alone in the dark
denied the warm light of the candles
the ancient smell of frankincense and myrrh.

The language is French,
and thrown on my own devices
I struggle the best I can in kindergarten.
A sheet is hung between two poles and
Voila! a puppet theater.
Our shoes are the puppets.
One by one the children
duck behind the sheet
put the shoes on their hands
hold them high up for all to see
and make them talk and sing:
"Ainsi font, font, font,
les petites marionnettes".
The nun never calls on me to sing.

I still have the little paper notebook,
the words "The Art Graphic" printed
elegantly on its now brittle brown cover.
I still see it on the wooden desk
I shared with a little boy who once peed in the classroom
a wet puddle spreading under us.
Sister was very angry.
Inside the book is my artwork;
a sailboat made of folded pink paper with a French flag
a sitting black cat torn from shiny black paper
two camels and a palm tree colored brown and green.
The word "Noel" with a candle.
Childish icons from a lost French civilization in the Congo.
How strange then, that my mother chose to pack it
and bring it back with her to New York
so I could now re-find it in Maltby.

To this day I love images of angels
blue veils with stars and halos
feathery wings on their shoulders.
They are the messengers.
I see them climbing the ladders between heaven and earth
their toes barely touching the rungs
as they rise upwards.
I see myself with wings.
I fly up into a golden sky
stars floating all around me
singing.

I've Never Seen a Madrone Tree
~~ Peggy Barnett – ©2012 ~~

A flock of birds flying together
landing in this town or the other
joining
separating
a black ribbon fluttering on the blue air,
their calls softly sung or loudly croaked
recognized by one another.
The one or two lone hawks are
committed to not eating the more fragile boned.

They fly in the orange sunset
landing on a madrone tree
or the roof of a crumbling arroyo house
on the side of the hot dusty road
a chicken running through one's feet
ready to be plucked
then dipped into bitter chocolate
for a few US dollars.

They fly over rock dark beaches
wild sucking waves
with dark fearsome shapes hunching
through the surface of the Pacific.
Bright hot heat of rocks
slowly turns into wet damp moss
as the river of words winds northward
always the orange setting sun beside them.

There are few thunderstorms here--
the ear shattering kind that breaks your bones
just the wind
a fearful wind
and the fire that consumes.

Faces here
turn to the lowering orb every evening
speaking words of finality and zen emptiness
the daily quenching of fire by water.
Poets walk into the waves
towards the round gold light
with their hands held before them
fingers disappearing
leaving green spots behind.

Where I was born I could see
the sun rise blue and cool every morning
across the black silver edged line of the Atlantic.
And the birds flew so fast
I hardly heard them call
but I saw them flying down the canyon walls of steel
across the hot asphalt
as the orange setting bouncing ball of a sun set
squeezed between two hard black skyscrapers
like a heart beating in a breathless chest.
Words fell out of windows
to be carried on the black backs of ravens
landing on trembling sunflowers.

The endlessly unrelenting every day dawn
began the hard sidewalk pounding
work of words,
old years firing up kilns across rusty iron bridges
down to where the dead suck sugared limes
north to where granite faced poets
fall off mountains
crushing cool sweet smelling balsams.

The Creekside

Of a summer evening
on a soft warm white sanded beach
a blue chill wind blows dark clouds
that shadow us.
Sadly packing our blankets
painfully donning sandpaper shoes
we run home before the dark falls down.

I stand on the shore
cold salty waves lapping at my feet
both there
and here.

Meditation on a Lost Cat

~~ Peggy Barnett – ©2011 ~~

At night I hear the tic-tic-tic of his nails on the wooden floor
his shadow passes through a reflected light.
His soul hovers at the door
which I did not open to let him in
in time.
A small life
self-involved
always touching, touching
to say I am here
to say you are here
we exist
no more is necessary.
If I could only hold onto that thought
I could move myself on through the night
and not keep waiting for the tic-tic-tic of his nails.

There is a tap-tap-tap that is beyond human
a universal touch on my lips
that wakes me up in the early morning
that accepts getting up and washing your face
without doubt.
As I get older I question less
the search for meanings gets weaker
more tiresome.
I'm evolving into a small soul
relieved to not need answers anymore.
But the why of it
the why of it
stays with me tap-tap-tap on my shoulder.

My garden's dark soil has no more dig-dig-dig for slugs
not even an orange body to bury.
Gone into the thin air
I breathe in his last life outside
in the winter cold
inhaling my lost warmth.
I watch the trees sway
the wet green grass turn brown
accepting the lesson of my aloneness.
It's only a cat
and it's only a little life
but it's the same life that we all share that's out there
surrounding us and through us.
I have my own allotment for a while until
eventually
it becomes time to dig-dig-dig for me.

The Thrift Store
~~ Peggy Barnett – ©2011 ~~

"No, you can't have it Ron."
"But it's solid brass. At least three pounds."
"It's too ugly."
"It" is a four inches long by three inches high
brass rabbit that's been made into a stapler.
"It's only $3.99. That's really cheap for all that brass."
"If it was solid gold, OK,
but I don't need a big brass rabbit stapler in the house.
That's final."
"You're very unreasonable."

My daughter and her boyfriend
wander the aisles searching for old clothes
the only acceptable attire in Portland
which they tear apart, cut, resew.
I think it's admirable;
except for the shoes.

Once, in an outdoor flea market in Manhattan
a big hubbub arose in a corner.
The word spread quickly;
"Parker died! He died in his booth. Parker's dead."
In minutes
like the old women in Zorba the Greek
the booth was stripped clean.
After the ambulance left
Ron picked up a worn library stool
lying tilted over on the asphalt.
We took it home
where it still remains
a memorial to every old Mr. Parker.

So Ron and I spend our older years
recycling our dishes and our fears.
I recycle my memories of life in New York
into poems
hoping they will someday
be of interest to someone else
who picks up my book in a thrift store.

The Glass
~~ Peggy Barnett – ©2011 ~~

In the back of my kitchen cabinet
there's an old candle glass holding
sixty years
of transparent memories.

My mother went to the temple to pray for the dead.
She never went for any other reason.
She only went to pray for the dead.
She didn't go for any joyous holidays.
She only went to pray for the dead
coming home with Grandma dressed in black
her eyes red, puffy.
She never took me to festivals
or to light candles on the Sabbath.

The only candles she lit were the Yahrzeit candles
in the glass with the arches pressed into a pattern
around the side.
At various times of the year,
two or three lights flickered and glowed in the
kitchen
an altar to deathdays
set up on a glass tray
on the thickly painted white wooden counter
over the drawer of old mismatched silver.
Orange flames glowed on five year old cheeks
staring at the glasses at night
scaring me with the shadows of dead people
moving and swaying on the kitchen ceiling
and walls behind me
reaching for me from some horrendous dark past.

After the wax had been burned away
we used the glasses to drink
Hines Black Cherry Soda
a little something sweet
to have after death.

Music
~~ Lil Buck – ©2013 ~~

Music is in the air
Music is in the air
Peace on earth may have a start
If we all keep music in our hearts.

My Furry Friend

~~ Lil Buck – ©2013 ~~

I have a furry, furry friend.
Her coat is soft and gray.
Her eyes are green and sometimes gold,
And such a joy to hold.

Sometimes when I am sad and lonely,
She greets me with her love.
She welcomes all my friends and neighbors,
They love her too.
To have a friend like her is priceless.
Her name is Babe.

The Secret Life of the Nose

~~ Terry Busch – ©2013 ~~

I stooped to smell an English rose
"The Heritage," she said
with pride and a knowing air

I closed my eyes and pulled its smell
into my nostrils and further still
to fill my mind with colors and memories

I stood six years old in my grandma's garden
where it seems that all her roses
held that aromatic intoxication

This was the first time in many
years that I have had this experience
as if roses had lost their scent for the sake of color

But maybe it is more that our sense of smell
always the handmaid to taste
has become the least of our perceptive skills

The dog, that master of the olfactory
plows bravely into that world following his nose
with no judgment of good or bad

We hold back avoiding the fetid
keeping it in reserve for "Is this leftover OK?"
and "Does the baby need changing?"

The nose can't lie even if it wanted to
It likes what it likes; avoids what it doesn't
and keeps its secrets

When I came back after living three months
in Mexico, I realized that my own country
had no pungency about it

We seem to be aware of this in the Northwest
As we drive our streets with open windows
every few blocks there is the smell of coffee

Lighthouse Keepers
~~ Terry Busch – ©2013 ~~

As a child I wanted to be a keeper

Over the years I've seen many lighthouses
on the Sound, along the Pacific, the Gulf
the Atlantic and around Lake Michigan

Poets are not unlike the keepers
of those stately beacons
drawn to the edges and places of solitude
aiming their beams of perception
into the murky unsettled regions
both exterior and interior
with hopes of bringing light there

And like those custodians of safety
there is a lot of down time
in which to walk around and think
appearing to others as being idle
but to the poet it is all study
a time of gathering together
and then bringing clarity

Before dawn
~~ Terry Busch – ©2013 ~~

I have given the wind my pledge. - Everett Ruess

There was a time and time again
when and where I found myself
alone watching the graying coals
die down in a solitary campfire

The night beyond its humble reach
has no pale blush of city lights
a purest black where stars sing out
each with its own bright voice

In that time in those distant places
usually cradling a broken heart
I make my way back to my self
finding only cold comfort in the dark

I sleep fitfully with the wind whipping
the tent to awaken me to a false dawn
then to struggle with a new fire
coffee my only companion

Now it is all fading memory
in those earliest of hours where
I have awakened too soon
with no care to know the time

I count those past camps and fires
to drowse and drift back to sleep
the wind now playing its sad notes
on my window screen far from the wild

Even now with my truest love beside me
there remains in me that quite place where
coals burn down in a vast desert with its night
as I once again await the coming dawn

Dancing on the Milky Way
~~ Terry Busch – ©2013 ~~

I prefer the mythos of the scientific
of atomic particles and the possibilities
of their nature where God is the details

We (this particular manifestation of atoms)
comes from some catastrophe of stars
billions of years long ago and far away

These atoms that are you and I
and the surrounding furniture and outside world
don't change much if at all over time

Without our perceptive projection
they would be abuzz like bees without a hive
a state of everything busily being everything

With open eyes to the spin of our black hole
which I first dreaded (light can't even escape)
we live with the spiral (nautilus to nebula)

This graceful form even informs the DNA helix
causing us to spin and spin like dervishes in time
dancing to a music we don't hear but live

The Red Wind
~~ Terry Busch – ©2013 ~~

*The white man will never be alone. Let him be just and deal kindly with
my people, for the dead are not powerless.*-Chief Seattle

The day Chief Leschi mounted the scaffold
the air was cold and clear

He could smell the fresh cut boards
beneath his bare feet

He knew that his people, the Nisqually
were safe but hungry on Fox Island
where they had been taken by the soldiers
to keep them separated from him

He had fought a cruel war to keep
the land that they had always lived on
but it was good land, in a good place
and the white men wanted it

He could see that the winter was fading
and that the snow geese heading North
would soon be filling the sky
and that the salmon were
out at sea and would soon return

Most things remained the same
His people would now have to make
their own way without him

He was the last in a line of chiefs
It was not meant for him to be a war chief
but there had been no choice

Now that he was to die
his people would be allowed
to return to live on the river

The floor opened beneath him
and the rope sang in his ears

His people came and cut him down
and took him to a place in the forest
where no one would ever find him

Limited

~~ Dennis Caswell – ©2012 ~~

The model train magazines he read after he retired
advertised little seats and painted vacationers

you could buy to trick out your passenger cars.
Upgrade your couplers! Spackle a hillside!

Add some more little trees, little ducks,
little hobos around little campfires.

The pages framed worlds of devotion
the way his black-and-white Zenith

could fit the Wide World of Sports
onto a nine-inch screen.

The full-scale giants who lived outside
would have to bend low

to look through his fifth-floor window
and see him sit on his bench of a couch,

completely authentic, as old
apartment 501 rattled around

the same short loop of years,
into the tunnel, out of the tunnel,

passing the pond, the barn, the depot
where all the painted people get off.

Credit: *Phlogiston*, Floating Bridge Press, 2012

An Experiment
~~ Dennis Caswell – ©2011 ~~

If the universe really is made
out of umpty-dimensional squiggles,
it's only because some physicist already had
those very squiggles inside his head,
and isn't that every scientist's dream:
to look at the whole universe
and see his own mind, the way a teenager looks
at the teeth and the hair and the powdery cheeks
and wet eyes of the pop stars who paper
her bedroom walls and sees herself,
her private, hormonal yearnings,
made larger, made radiant, made flesh.
Back in the '60's (the 1760's), one Thomas Day
decided his ideal bride had never been born
and therefore must be made, so he popped on down
to the Orphan Asylum at Shrewsbury,
plucking himself an auburn brunette
called Sabrina, age eleven, whom he undertook
to breed up into himself
as a beautiful girl. And yet, in spite of Sabrina's
"engaging countenance" and "the uncommon melody
of her voice," after a year, he let her go,
finding her to be less mirror than window
onto a cosmos governed by laws
he couldn't have written. He sent her
to boarding school, paid a substantial dowry
when she married, and when her husband died

24

gave her a small allowance the rest of her life,
keeping the kind of place in his heart for her
my mother still keeps for John Barrymore
or that a scientist keeps for a colleague
who's proven him wrong.

*The story of Thomas Day in "An Experiment" was taken from the essay
"The Author of 'Sanford and Merton'" by John Fyvie, found in the
book* A Clutch of Curious Characters, *edited by Richard Glyn Jones.
The story has been somewhat simplified. In addition to Sabrina, Mr.
Day found a second girl, Lucretia, at the Foundling Hospital in
London. His plan was to educate them both for a year, then select the
most suitable one and continue to educate her, with a view toward
marriage when she became of age. The girl not chosen would be
apprenticed to a "reputable tradeswoman." Lucretia, described by an
acquaintance of Mr. Day as "invincibly stupid," was duly apprenticed
to a milliner and eventually married a respectable linendraper.*

Credit: Journal *Vain*, 2011

Preservation

~~ Dennis Caswell – ©2012 ~~

Watching a bagpiper gather his gawky bundle of sticks
and bladders against his body like something run over—
its organs and bones hanging out—and give it mouth-to-mouth,
then hearing it bleat to life like a baby dinosaur
born with a wonky septum, I want to take them both home
in a shoe box and feed them from an eyedropper. Once,
in an animal park, I saw a birdcage
labeled so as to inform me
that the ounce of jitter it contained
was the last dusky seaside sparrow on earth,
and they were damn well going to keep it alive
until it exploded into dust. Of the 6,900-odd
human languages, 20 are currently spoken
by only one person. I feel responsible.
I want to give them their ancestors back
the way zoologists tried resurrecting the quagga
by breeding back from zebras,
the way musicians abjure underwear
while training their giant Jurassic spiders
to wheeze "Amazing Grace" on command,
and now that I think of it marching bands
should play "Louie, Louie" on Renaissance sackbuts,
racketts and shawms, and every house should bear a plaque
that lists every person who ever slept there.
Every name should be carved in granite somewhere.

Credit: Journal, *Fault Lines*, 2012

Remains

~~ Dennis Caswell – ©2012 ~~

"Good morning, my beautiful children, god *damn*
but your mother was dynamite in the ol' sack last night!"

numbers among the things my father never said,
along with "Crank up the Hendrix!" and "I've been
thinking it over,

and that Martin King might just have a point." In fact,
there weren't many things he *did* say as he buried himself

in his easy chair beneath a glacier of nicotine
and muscatel on the rocks. Yet somehow,

while he was under there, he put me through college,
handing out checks from under the layers of ice

so I could learn whole libraries full
of things he would never say, embrace ideas

he despised, appreciate art a dog could have made,
acquire respect for the kinds of people who ought to be

lined up and shot, though he never said that either.
That's my reconstruction, like when a paleontologist

looks at a handful of blunted teeth and imagines
a weed-grinding lizard who never saw the asteroid coming,

or when an archeologist digs up a shard of clay
and envisions a civilization that once believed it had

a future, or when an astronomer finds a hole in space
and reckons back to an aging sun, out of fuel, imploding.

Credit: *Phlogiston*, Floating Bridge Press, 2012

Post-Modern Goddess
~~ Glenna Cook – ©2013 ~~

Like young Persephone, innocence still clings
to your round cheeks. You see world as new,
made just for your pleasure.

Like Athena, you're Daddy's smart girl.
Completing your masters with high GPA,
you're ready to march toward your dreams.

You're most like Artemis:
restless for travel, at home in Moscow or London,
fearlessly roaming the hills of Seattle.

Brown hair swings over black leather jacket,
heel of second-hand boot coming off,
hole in the toe of your tights,
keys in hand, as you stride a dark street.

A Man Plans Differently
~~ Glenna Cook – ©2012 ~~

than a woman for a journey.
He sees where he is going,
finds the shortest way to get there
and get back.

He takes two changes of underwear,
two extra shirts, two pair of pants,
a little bag of toiletries. Money.

A woman looks
at what is being left behind.

She cleans her house for coming home to.
All the people in her life
must be informed of where she's going,
when she will return.

Someone must be found to tend her plants
and care for her cat.

She packs three changes of clothes
for every change of weather,
bakes nut bread to eat along the way.

Elegy for a Shepherdess

~~ Glenna Cook – ©2012 ~~

From La Gardeuse de Moutons,
painted by William-Adolphe Bouguereau, 1881

How lovely the scene behind you,
for which you show no interest. Cliffs rise
above pasture where sheep graze.
Reddening shrubs, a river,
black hills in the distance.

What has harmed you, shepherd girl, that the quiet
oval of your face reflects the storm clouds
threatening to swallow the day?

You sit on a stone,
in homespun blues and grays. Golden curls
escape their scarf, fall onto slumped shoulders.
A large button fastens a vest over still
unblossomed breasts. Below your skirt,
shapely legs and bare feet cross at the ankle.

In one hand, an unfinished sock and knitting needles;
in your lap, a switch for nicking heels of wayward lambs.

Why are your lips so firmly set?
Gray eyes, too knowing for your age
look straight into mine.
I think you would tell me something,
if only you could trust.

Treasure Under Sri Padmanabhaswamy Temple

~~ Glenna Cook – ©2013 ~~

It takes multiple keys to unlock the three doors,
five strong men to move a marble slab. A stairway
leads down a dark and narrow passage
to treasure so vast it cannot be measured—
gold ornaments, heaps of gems,
coin from empires long since vanquished—
sacred property of Vishnu.

Once, a few stick-wielding temple workers
and a golden cobra, embossed above the vault door,
had protected it. Now that it has been seen,
two-hundred men guard it with machine guns.
Now that it has been seen,
a big dispute on how to spend it.

Through a door into your own psyche,
down another dark passage,
hidden and guarded,
a different kind of treasure awaits discovery.

Approach it at your own risk.
Once you have seen it,
you must decide how to spend it.
Once you have seen it,
nothing will ever be the same.

So Much Treading
~~ Glenna Cook – ©2010 ~~

No one can know, or needs to know,
how in the course of our long marriage
these safe paths were formed.
We have learned to walk around
briars and bogs, keep away
from edges of cliffs.

Along these paths that we have carved
by so much treading,
lie picked bones of contention.
More significant are the monuments
we've raised, rough cast, yet beautiful,
sacrificial altars built by raw hands
lifting stone upon stone.

Some, not knowing, wonder how we,
so different from each other,
could travel so long together.
We can't tell you. We only know that
time alone has taught which notes
sing well along the way,

No one knows, or needs to know,
the words to our own peculiar song.

Autumn

~~ Virginia B. Cook – ©2013 ~~

How light the heart as Summer fades to Fall
with asters and chrysanthemums in bloom,
and late clematis blooming on the wall
still fragrant as long autumn evenings loom.

The sun now rises later in the morn
and sets a minute earlier each eve,
and Summer sheds the green cloak she has worn
and counts the shrinking days til she should leave.

A shift in sunshine, changing taste of dew,
a sound of songbirds vacating their nests,
a briskness in the wind today from skies still blue
that marks the winged departing of wild summer guests.

Gardens are harvested; corn ripens on spent stalks.
Thus comes a new autumnal equinox.

Counting Stitches

~~ Virginia B. Cook – ©2011 ~~

Today I'm sewing doll clothes
for a project at our church
with scraps of fabric all around
and patterns I have searched.
I've found some lace and bias tape
and two kinds of elastic,
the doll waits on my sewing desk -
her smile fixed in plastic.

The sewing brings me back again
to scenes from long ago
when Mother sat at her machine
with things to mend or sew.
Her whitened hair and gentle eyes
I see across the years
while she assembled some surprise
for children she held dear.

I'm older now than she was then
and know how I was blessed,
of all the things she did for me
such caring was the best.
Like Mother, I'm surrounded now
by scissors, threads and pins.
Withdrawn from details in my life
that constantly push in.

But though this work is harder now
and stiffened fingers grope
to thread the needles' tinier eyes
I find I have the hope

That my own children will find ease
from modern living's stress
by working on some tasks like these
that bring content and rest.

Cat Tale

~~ Virginia B. Cook – ©2009 ~~

There was nothing quite as clever as the cat we had back home.
He groomed his catapult (pelt) with a little catacomb.
He climbed up caterpillars and sat down on catalogues.
The one thing on his catalyst was that he hated dogs.

For when he ever saw one he would catamount a tree
to avoid a cataclysmic scene of cat nip, don't you see?
He feared that dog would catch him and make him all category,
and he'd be cataleptic, just as well, and end this story.

So he sailed off in a catboat with one cat's paw on the tiller,
while drinking catatonic while his caterwaul grew shriller.
But it finally took catastrophe to make him catwalk back,
this doggerel was just too much for him to counteract.

Flash of Courage

~~ Virginia B. Cook – ©2004 ~~

Old Flash was the best of the ponies
in the Emsdale Colliery.
Never saw the like, from dawn to night
but a grand little pony was he.

He knew every inch of the coal ways
in the Emsdale Colliery,
and he knew that once his shift was done
he could rest to the morning free.

Lived in the mine with his stall mates
in this Yorkshire Colliery,
and they never knew of the outdoor view,
of the sun or grass or trees.

They pulled the heavy coal cars
through the maze of the Colliery.
T'was in years of yore so long before
these days of you and me.

The owner was losing money
from the Emsdale Colliery,
did at last decide to set the beasts aside
and use modern machinery.

The day that the coal cars were cabled
in the Emsdale Colliery,
The pony troop were all brought up
to be sent to the knackery.

Just then came a great explosion
in the works of the Colliery.

A ton of coal formed up a wall;
twenty men were in jeopardy.

There was just one living creature
knew the maze of the old Colliery,
so they took old Flash back down a shaft
to depend on his memory.

Flash trotted sll through the tunnels
of the worked-out Colliery,
and he brought them all to a dead- end wall:
just beyond it the men would be.

They rescued the men, but the pony
stayed down in the Colliery,
for the men and boys were so overjoyed
they forgot where Flash might be.

Flash ran to his stall in the stable
in the depths of the Colliery,
for he knew he won; now his work was done,
in his old home he would be.

The miners set out to fetch him
from the depths of the old Colliery,
but a second blast caused the death of Flash.
Even now they all agree:

Old Flash was the best of the ponies
in the Emsdale Colliery.
Never saw the like, from dawn to night,
but a grand little pony was he.

He knew every inch of the coal ways
in the Emsdale Colliery,
and he knew that once his shift was done
he could rest to the morning free.

A Different World

~~ Virginia B. Cook – ©2008 ~~

Although the path I've traveled has been long,
I cannot say I've learned all I should know.
Some wisdom I have gained by being wrong
with Rightness coming difficult and slow.

Some chapters of my life were filled with light
dissolving dark that did not want to go.
Sometimes the path ascended to a height
to bring me vision of the way to go.

And much of it has been in the same world -
familiar landmarks all around the place -
but lately it seems Destiny has hurled
me into unfamiliar Time and Space.

Has my perception somehow been deranged
or has our world become completely changed?

For Julie

~~ Mary Eliza Crane – ©2012 ~~

I savor the quiet and dark,
face turned up to a pattering mist
in a cold inscrutable sky.
A belly of leftover rice
tossed with onion and garlic,
hazel and walnut
raisins, orange and salt.

I savor the heart
of my troubled ancestral sister
bearing the breath of the dead in her bones.
Blown in like a bird,
she stayed for the trees,
the food, and warmth of the hearth.
The roar of the creek her unquenchable thirst
as our eyes start to pierce through the dark.

Grosbeaks

~~ Mary Eliza Crane – ©2012 ~~

Early morning wrapped in woven wool
white breath dissolving into fog,
one fawn lay supine near my feet
sweet docile sister grazing in the weeds.
Mother doe caught and held my gaze,
but bored by lack of threat
she drifted back away into the fog
my steaming teacup met, then glancing up
sunbeams crowned a cottonwood
that cast one patch of light
on the first golden leaves that drifted down.

Teacup empty, hot oats and milk consumed,
sky deep Nordic blue from a lover's eye,
on the smallest branch atop the tallest fir,
black headed cinnamon breasted
grosbeaks flock and call.
They take the best sun, and cast no shadow.
Unlike us, they leave some for tomorrow.

Credit: *"Quill and Parchment"*, Nov 2012

Picking Blueberries

~~ Mary Eliza Crane – ©2013 ~~

The morning wet with heavy dew,
late summer sun's low angled rays
crest above a row of cedars,
relieving chill. I seek out silence.
Nimble fingers sift for ripened berries
not too soft, but having lost
their rosy blush. It's slow, but to no mind,
while lost in time with agile hands.
Other pickers come in one by one
in family vans, children run with empty buckets
but somehow they can't find enough.
Last years were bigger better
some are old and some have mold,
while I calmly rove from bush to bush.

A child whines that this is work,
her mother reassures that work is good.
This isn't work,
it's a weekend morning in the sun.
This isn't famine food.
No one is eating bark
or holding hungry children in the dark.

This is blots of blue with melted butter,
maple syrup, buckwheat flour,
Sunday morning pancake breakfast.

Primroses

~~ *Mary Eliza Crane* – ©*2012* ~~

The winter after
my father in law died
darkened with an angry
unspeakable, unreachable grief.
I too stayed silent
tongue tied into a glottal stop
that choked back every
tone and timbre,
every hunger, sorrow, need.
Days dawned in pounding sheets
staccato leaden gray,
folded back into a starless rainy black.

I found a wilder river.
Strewn with slippery boulders,
foaming rapids raging danger
beat a mist upon my face.
My heart relinquished,
I sang discordant to the wind.

Each week,
one tame yellow primrose
came home from the grocery store,
an open hand of color
beneath the blackened skies.
Some lived. Most barely did.

That spring is as far away
as my father in law and his son.
After a chilling frost,
the flesh of my toes sprawl
and sink into damp grass,
under a warm and sensuous sun.

45

My throat opens up
and swallows the sky.

Poem for the Northeastern Woods

~~ Mary Eliza Crane – ©2011 ~~

This is mine, she said,
thirty five years from her angry departure
drawn to the sound of a cold mountain brook.

Her smile came slowly,
toes plunged in fresh water surrounded by hellebore
acres of trout lily standing in birch,
viburnum, red trillium
wind gusting bare branches
woodpecker drumming dead oak for a mate.

Her mother is old.
The carpets ripped up reveal fine ancient flooring,
it might be the last time she walks in the house.

Blue sky penciled the first words she spoke,
followed by freedom
while seeking the truth that eluded:

This earth could take her in.

John Wayne
~~ Larry Crist – ©2013 ~~

was tough
was tender
had small feet
walked that certain way
Smoked 4 packs a day
drank more than he ought
always knew his lines
Missed the big war
fought the cold one
Considered movie content
more important than the role
Character had but one meaning
Never played a villain
Adored his father
Never felt much love from his mother
Was a man's man
Had a thing for crazy Latino women
Made 177 movies
89 westerns
16 combat
18 John Ford films
—the man he called Pappy
Loved his country
Hated commies
Beat cancer
till it beat him
Won one for True Grit

Not bad for a fourth string tackle
out of San Pedro

Tarzan

~~ Larry Crist – ©2013 ~~

Elmo Lincoln
played him first
1918: they brought in a sick elderly lion
from Griffith Park
fixed his claws so he couldn't scratch
shot it full of dope
Barrel-chested Elmo jumped on it
as the hand cranked camera rolled
Stabbed it and stood on it
Planted his foot on its rib cage
Beat his chest, performing that jungle yodel
for the first time
as rancid gas squeezed through the lion's wounds
telling Elmo there'd be no second take

Elmo complains from the rest home that all those who followed
were really just pussy swimmers, fags in loin clothes
who cupped their cries, smote their waxed chests
shaved their arm pits and faces, everything
talked too much, wore little moccasins
lived with women and communed with monkeys
used gel in their hair

Elmo confesses the trees he swung through were only eight feet
    tall
and once while filming in Louisiana
he accidentally fell into a swamp with a real live alligator
and had no choice but to fight

They kept rolling
while another Tarzan
shaved in the wings

The Mentor
~~ Larry Crist – ©2013 ~~

My old writing teacher
older now
and plenty old then
hunched over his beer
creases form between the rim of his glasses
and the brim of his cap
his keen eyes observant through the thick reflective glass
that overwhelm his short sharp nose

He is working on something
and can't get an agent
his old one died or something
he can't really drink or smoke anymore either
He said he had writer's block for 5 years once
after having quit cigarettes
I don't know what else he can or cannot do
He cannot stay and has to go

He knows i have adopted him
perhaps he is honored
maybe annoyed
but he has always been a good teacher
and like the bubbles in our glasses
he rises to the occasion

You keep going, he orders.
You keep at it and fight those bastards.
You do it because you must.

He stands
his small wizened body towers
I rise as well and nearly topple, having sat too long on one leg

Wobbly from drinking that which he cannot
He catches me and we share a clumsy embrace

He exits the dark bar into the day
and i have another
to him

Mexican Ferris Wheel
~~ Larry Crist – ©2013 ~~

We were in some little town in Mexico
It was dark and we were slightly drunk
returning to the hotel where we were staying
when we happened upon a carnival
There were rides and carney side-shows
and we wandered past spinning-twirling cups
and a revolving capsule gizmo
and a pathetic shot-up looking Merry-go-round
decapitated horses and busted up figures
and food offerings that would no-doubt have
made us sick, and having looked over everything else
we came to a Ferris Wheel, that i talked her into getting on
We were the only ones who wanted to ride it
The attendant placed a screwdriver through the catch to prevent
it from opening and released a large lever and we crept
backward to the top where we could look over the carnival
and the not much bigger town. Look, i laughed, our
lives are held in check by a screwdriver. And who knows,
what little else, she said, that will keep us from dying?
See those pigs in their pen. That's where we
would tumble were we to fall, I said.
That probably wouldn't kill us, she said—it would
make quite a story though.
We stayed up at the top longer than we would have
on a busier, safer Norte-American wheel
The attendant, i figured, had resumed drinking in the cantina
    next door
and maybe we would have to climb down or perhaps the wheel
would break loose and we'd start rolling forward or worse…
The screwdriver rattled in its slot as i rocked us
back and forth which she immediately made me stop
We were too married to make-out
but took in the magic of the stars and a dim looking planet

neither of us could identify
And when again we began to move
it felt like we had been somewhere
instead of in a big loop through space
The pigs chortled as we passed them
engrossed in their slops
It was good to walk among them upon the earth again

Primitive Porn
~~ Larry Crist – ©2013 ~~

It was long ago
Hef was dating gals his own age
Larry Flynt was but a kid in Tennessee
exploring bestiality
and i was in a bookstore with my father
where we'd browse, ignoring
the *this-is-not-a-library* sign
I don't know what my father was looking at
but i had 10¢ and it was always a tough call
between Sad Sack and Hot Stuff
Then IT caught my eye
gals in ripped shirts and bras and panties and garters and
     stockings
tied up and strapped down
some with whips and on one cover
chucking grenades and firing machine guns

It looked like they were fighting World War Two
they were battling nazis and Japanese in any case

My father had been reading me a history of World War Two
he would read and then explain what he had read
it was all very complicated
somewhere between the failure of Versailles
and the invasion of Poland
and the dropping of the atomic bomb
there was a lot to cover
but i don't recall anything about these women
obviously brave and courageous
and pretty well-fed too
with their clothes giving out in all the right places
for it was better to imagine those places
along side those exposed areas

bound by rope and chain
tattered and bruised and desperate with just a dab or hint of
    blood
leered at and slobbered upon
by buck-toothed Japanese in glasses
stocky krauts with scars and eye patches

One didn't need to be an historian
or even an adult
to know what this war was about

And as soon as i began to look
i knew i wasn't supposed to
I could only imagine the fate of the girls
and whether i ended up buying Sad Sack or Hot Stuff
i could not forget these tough gorgeous women
these victorious vixens
who looked nothing like mom
or my friend's moms
or my teachers or
sunday school teachers
or the girls at school
or anybody on television even
nobody looked like these women
who were of course illustrations
but oh-so real
so very real

World War Two was a lot more interesting than dad or
Winston Churchill had been letting on
and maybe that particular war was over
but a new one was beginning
and i had but a few more years
to prepare

Catalogs

~~ Clark Crouch – ©2004 ~~

We're really lost without it,
our mail order store,
now that Monkey Ward is gone
don't get catalogs no more.

They was pretty good reading,
them catalogs of theirs
stuff we've always wanted
and answers to our prayers.

They filled a lot of evenings
when snow lay on the hills
and offered entertainment,
respite from winter's chills.

When a new catalog came
the old would be sent away
to the outhouse out in back...
recycled, so they say.

Monkey Ward went belly up,
no catalogs to issue
so they've been superseded
by rolls of toilet tissue.

Credit: *Where Horses Reign,* 2004

Goose Creek

~~ Clark Crouch – ©2007 ~~

The creek meanders listlessly
amidst the hills of sand…
a shallow, slender thread of life
feeding the fragile land.

It brings water to our cattle
and makes the meadows green
with grasses as tall as a man
as far as can be seen,

Willow branches droop o'er the stream,
shading the water's flow,
creating quiet, cool retreats
where man is wont to go.

This little creek flows steadily
as seasons rise and wane,
grandly fulfilling its purpose,
in this prairie domain.

Credit:_Western Images, 2007
Honorable Mention, Thirteenth Juried Poetry Reading,
Allied Arts of Yakima Valley, 2007

The Guardian

~~ Clark Crouch – ©2004 ~~

It was a lonely hilltop
where the prairie grasses played,
tossed by the winds of summer
and barren of any shade.

From that grand promontory
one could see a distant home
rising from the prairie sod
and the land where cattle roam.

To the west the land stretched on...
waves of grass, a moving sea,
splashing on a sandy shore
too distant for man to see.

The river, off to the south,
shrunken from the springtime flood
with waters now running blue,
and no longer filled with mud.

But that view was overcome
by a mound of new-turned soil
and a wee fist of daisies
that marked a poor digger's toil.

Guarding that lonely hilltop
a small home-made cross now stands,
marking one more sacrifice
to hardship on prairie lands.

The sod home seemed empty then
but the rancher toiled on
glancing very frequently
t'ward the place his love'd gone.

Credit: *Where Horses Reign,* 2004

The Historian

~~ Clark Crouch – ©2009 ~~

Jeffrey just showed up one Fall day
and made himself to home,
seems like he was too old to work
and now too tired to roam.

He was willin' to do some chores
and did odd jobs each day...
cleanin' out the stalls in the barn
and tossin' out some hay.

But what old Jeff enjoyed doin'
was talkin' to young folks,
sharin' wondrous, magical yarns...
all true, he said, no jokes.

Jeff'd sit down and light his pipe
and peer through half-closed eyes
and then recite the oft-told tales,
swearin' that none were lies.

He'd stood on the shore at Jamestown
givin' a welcome hand
to John Smith and the colonists
as they came on this land.

And if you'd look, he said you'd see
the mark he did affix
declarin' our independence
back in seventy-six.

He'd wintered at the Yellowstone
and trapped with mountain men,

bringin' in a furry fortune
'fore headin' out again.

He had fought at the Alamo
with Davy Crockett's band
and escaped from Santa Anna
down south in Texas land.

Durin' the Civil War he served
with Robert Edward Lee
and pursued the Union Army,
forced it into the sea.

He was at the Little Big Horn
and barely saved his hair
by escapin' from the Indians
who fought with Custer there.

But we hear Jeffrey's tales no more
because he passed away.
His epitaph's on yonder hill,
he has no more to say.

What grain of truth in what he said?
What matter there was none,
for he brought a sense of wonder
that can n'er be undone.

Credit: *Views from the Saddle,* 2009

61

The Reign of St. Helens

~~ Clark Crouch – ©2003 ~~

On this spring morning
everything seemed quite normal.
The earth did grumble a bit,
and sent tell-tale wisps of smoke
from fissures on the mountain
many miles westward.

But here, dawn was bright and clear
heralding another day...
Sunday, a day of leisure,
one to be enjoyed;
a day of worship,
one for which to be thankful.

The early morning
bursting with voices...
birds singing their songs;
muffled voices of neighbors,
heard but indistinct;
the sounds of traffic,
from the highway to the south;
a lawn mower starting up;
a dog barking right next door...
normal voices for Sunday.

Then a deadening silence
seemed to swallow up the earth.
The voices were silent
and the air was quiet, still,
no whisper of wind.
Birds were not flying
nor were they singing.
The dog hid under the porch.

Dark clouds moved in from the west,
covering the sky,
bringing an eerie darkness.

Udder-like appendages
laden with volcanic ash
hung below the clouds,
sifting out fine ash
to cover the landscape
and burden the roofs of homes.

Mount St. Helens had spoken,
pushed aside man's monuments,
and declared her sovereignty.

Credit: *Reflections,* 2003

Super Star

~~ Dorothy Dean – ©2013 ~~

Under the sudden spotlight's glare
Her tresses don't look wash and wear
The crowd grows wild and whistles while
She gleams her dazzling porcelain smile

Her luscious lashes, lips that shine
Are thanks to Helen Rubenstein
It matters little if she sings
With bosoms built like water wings
At least I'm sure they are her own
Paid for in full (and silicone)

Her eighteen hour girdle holds
In place her over-ample folds,
All praise to sound men in control
Electron-rich, her voice has soul.
She gets her cue, sways sensually
Begins to sing, "I gotta be me."

Volcano

~~ Dorothy Dean – ©2013 ~~

Now this seems how world's end will be
St. Helens trembles. From some deep
And secret core, a blast, one roar
Of anguish, spewing pluming clouds
Roiling, spreading, strangely flooding out
All light from west to east, taking night
To the height of noon. A breathless, waiting silence
Grows. Then soon comes softly falling rain
Of dead, grey ash. The following day's
A moonscape. Dust shrouds every thing.
And no bird flies.
And no bird sings.

Late Harvest

~~ Dorothy Dean – ©2013 ~~

Neglected on the kitchen table
lies a scribbled seedling poem,
while in the bean patch
a false-summer sun spreads warmth
across my bent back.

With rough, brown fingers,
I probe for smooth, green ones
concealed in a confusion of leaves
already crisp with fall.

But late beans, like late words,
no longer come easily
after summer's extravagance is spent.

Now I thrust through tangles
for discovery –
one savory phrase that sings.

The poem puts forth slow, tentative lines,
yet on these vines,
white blossoms lift bright faces
with parted lips,
expectant
but ignorant
of winter.

Scorn-of-Plenty
~~ Dorothy Dean – ©2013 ~~

Once cavemen tracked their daily fare,
Then, with great derring-do,
Speared tiger, mastodon or bear
And held a barbeque.

They gnawed upon each knucklebone
And odds and ends botanic,
Assured in knowing these had grown
By processes organic.

Obtaining chow is safer now.

Into each shopping cart
Goes foodstuff, all well-fortified
with nitrates, dyes, insecticide,
and vinyl-wrapped. We've turned the tide.
To eat's the risky part.

Battery Included

~~ Dorothy Dean – ©2013 ~~

An electrical eel
In search of a meal
Has manners most shockingly rude.
Yet this slow-swimming fryer
Requires no wire
To sizzle and frizzle her food.

How amazing to glide
With a battery inside
For she may not be clever or cunning.
Though her charms don't bewitch,
Once she turns on the switch,
At six hundred volts,
She is stunning

Antique Store
~ J. Glenn Evans – ©2007 ~

An ancient clock bongs for a grandfather
Who hears and sees no more
A crude wooden horse carved for a child
By a father long ago, whose son is now gone
Glasses toasted at family gatherings
Rugs felt stocking feet that tread no more

Ashtrays for folks who smoked too much
Depression and war weary
Who listened to Roosevelt's fireside chats
Pictures and glass and furniture
Knickknacks and jewelry a thousand choices
From a thousand homes, cherished by someone

Tables and chairs of those who broke bread
Will never find their places again
Whose lips have touched these cups
What child played with this doll
What baby sat in this high chair
What proud hostess served tea with this silver set

Only these antiques know
So carefully chosen, so easily disposed
A thousand treasures carry the spirit
Of those who touched, waiting and waiting
At the antique store for proud new owners
To cherish once more

Credit*: Dan River Anthology*—2007
Backstreet Review--#25-Jul/2009

My Grandfather Spoke

~~ J. Glenn Evans – ©2003 ~~

When I was young my grandfather spoke
Told me things I did not understand
We sat cross-legged and faced each other
Under a blackjack oak tree out in the field
Day was warm and sunny under blue sky
Redbird in the tree chirped its song
Grasshoppers and butterflies flew about

As we sat there my grandfather said to me
My son I am old, I will not be long
The earth cries for our wisdom
Most of the bear are now no more
No Buffalo roam free
Fox and Wolf have no place to go
These things were many when I was young

My grandfathers were unwise men
They welcomed invaders as friends and gods
When they came to know this was foolish
They fought and argued among themselves
The enemy grew stronger and we grew weaker
Many died from white man's sickness
Now too late to fight we are beaten

We are few and they are many
Bear and Buffalo are gone
Fox and Wolf have no place to go
Time will come when only the foolish rule
And their foolish ways destroy
They will bring great sickness upon the land
I hear the earth cry for our wisdom

You must learn to lead these people my son
Love and protect this place that is our home
Room for Bear and Wolf and all people
Years have passed since my grandfather spoke
I know what he was trying to tell me
They cannot her my grandfather's voice
I hear the earth cry for our wisdom

Credit: *All Night Diner*-18Oct05
Buffalo Tracks, SCW Publications, 2003

Napoleon

~~ J. Glenn Evans – ©2005 ~~

In Seattle I sit and watch the rain
Wash down upon the city's core
And I think of you on that rock, St. Helena
Looking out the window at the rain

I've read your diary and notes on glory
Were those your real thoughts, or just PR?
You could have been a Cromwell of Europe
Set the stage for a true democracy

What if you had made the rule of France
Exemplary of how best to rule
For the benefit of all the people
Would citizens then have cause to burn castles?

You'd had your glory without cannon
We might know the names of those who died
Those who perished in the Russian snow
Those who fought for you and against you

Did you give a thought to all the men
Who perished in the Russian snow
The van Goghs, the Poes, the Picassos,
Whose names we shall never know

You sit on the rock of St. Helena and gaze at the rain
That cleaned their wounds and drained away their hopes
The same rain that now falls on Seattle
Rain that reminds me of other lives lost for glory

Credit: *Poetic Voices Without Borders-Gival Press-*2005
*Clark Street Review-All Night Diner-*Dec/05

Old Man's Winter
~~ J. Glenn Evans – ©2013 ~~

After Theodore Roethke (1908-1963)

To take, to take—
I feel that mist.
As though my boiler was busted
I think my bones forgot.
Like half-gone love I hug my memories.
O for a vision of what's to come,
Heavenly music across the bay,
Echo of the Lord's message,
Full jolly, a string
Melodious and,
On the straightaway
Lost among the firs and wood songs
Wind flashes by
To hold conference with me
Where mountains converse,
And leap over shoulders,
Of an old man
Racing like a fool.
If only I could go back
To gather memories holding sway,
Coming back this way,
The passions of my day,—
Floating on a sea of memories
In a house of beautiful memories
Now that time is gone:
I'm old and life is done

Credit: *Washington State Poet Laureates Web Site*

The Trespass

~~ J. Glenn Evans – ©2003 ~~

Parked my car in front of Grandpa's old place
Pear trees all gone but stump of a fallen one
Old well with gourd for passing strangers
Now just bare ground and covered hole

Locked rusty iron gate barred my way
I climbed over and walked up to the old house
Trees along the fencerow were the same old oaks
But fence posts and barbwire were missing

Old house stood nude of shingles
Roof joists a skeleton against the sky
Covered porch fallen down and carried away
Living room floorboards broken and rotted

Where once Grandpa and I listened
To Joe Louis fights and Edward R. Murrow's
War news from England Sicily invasion
About our victories and our defeats

Old wood stove where we warmed ourselves
And told stories around no longer there
Grandpa's living room now looked so small.
How could all of us have fit there

Grandma's porcelain sink, cracked and broken
Still there but not the old cook stove
Where she baked vanilla cookies
When she saw her grandchildren coming

Out back the old hickory tree
Which I had leaned against at age four

Upchucked my first drink of whisky
I had pestered grandpa to give me

This old hickory tree that shaded the yard
Filled my pockets with hickory nuts
Had now fallen with its arms
Laid at rest across roof of this old house

I looked up the path through the woods
Where Grandma and I picked Polk salad
Then I walked up to her old garden spot
Looked north across an open field

Once we raised corn and cotton here
Now the field was covered with grass
But in the center remained an old oak
That I once climbed when I was young

Though it was summer, spring wild flowers
Still danced in the breeze out in the field
I walked up to that old oak tree
Climbed it again and then went home

Credit: *First place winner in The Rock River Poetry Contest* 2003
First published in The Rock River Times, Rockford IL

November Tritina
~~ Kathleen Flenniken – ©2012 ~~

November is a necklace of daytime headlights
crossing the floating bridge. Silk
breast of a winter wren, scarf tied loosely at the neck. It's
    the sun

or more correctly, its lack. No, you're my sun,
parsing the fog, light
spun and suspended in a web. November is a grey silk

suit, white shirt, dark silk
tie with a wine stain, Sun-
day coat, all in a pile, headlight

beams through a scrim and a distant horn. Light head, silky
    breath, sun going down.

Previously published in *Alaska Quarterly Review*

News Item
~~ Kathleen Flenniken – ©2012 ~~

New research suggests we have
a fixed reservoir of self-restraint.

This is why at the end of the day
you smuggle bowls of ice cream to the TV

Or put another way
when you pushed your plate aside
and hunger kneaded your gut for months
this is why you crammed the closet with new clothes
and emerged from your diving bell
in a breathless hotel room
why you let the coat fall from your shoulders

That manic week
when you ironed every shirt and tablecloth
why you couldn't keep up with the grief

Last night sirens passed close
this morning the airwaves crash and moil
and your mail is flooded with catalogs

This is why you've staged your house like a catalog
why you can't bear to open the bills
why streets are jammed with luxury cars
and panhandlers
and your country is at war

Previously published in *Tar River Poetry*

Center Square

~~ Kathleen Flenniken – ©2013 ~~

Why was Paul Lynde so funny?
I laughed but not like the studio audience

who laughed too long and loud
at expressions and a voice that stretched

and buzzed like an accordion.
He was funny like a fist is funny

painted with a face. He was center square,
the "tac" in tic-tac-toe,

the handsome-ish player
with the snarkiest bluff and biggest

applause. He could be mean, easy to mimic,
master of hilarious and puzzling one-liners

and I too young to shock.
I liked it best when time was short

or he wasn't in the mood to joke and his answer
came out serious, like a kaleidoscope

when the colors line up and the image
is briefly clear. I could see all the way into

his darkness. I could love him, I thought,
and fix him, if only he'd play it straight,

which said everything about my ignorance
of the heart—mine and his

and mine.

Previously published in *Clover, A Literary Rag*

Buried Alive
(Copiapo, Chile)
~~ *William Scott Galasso – ©2012* ~~

At La Esperanza, (Camp Hope), the vigil goes on.
Interminable, this day. So near, so far. They wait,
mothers, wives and daughters as they have for days,
weeks, months nerves frayed as rope too long used
and chafing. Emotions raw as oysters drawn fresh
and dripping from the sea, holding candles, praying
for loved ones, praying to Mary, Saint Jude, anyone
that will listen for fathers, sons, and brothers.

And down below they wait each minute an hour,
each hour a day. Dirty, hungry, sleeping in the dark
that knows no sun. Dreaming of all the things they
took for granted, solid food perhaps, a sip of Pisco*,
the touch of a wife's hand or their child's laughter.
They listen, hear the scrape and moan of drill,
the sound of rescue. They are not forgotten,
not abandoned. Their comrades will not give up.

One by one they're lifted up, modern Lazarene's
receiving the light's benediction, reborn to hope
love and a new way of seeing.

If you ever question, the true cost of gold, think
of the miners below.

*Pisco, the national drink of Chile, made from muscat
 grapes. Copiapo is the site of the San Jose' copper mine.

Credit: *Collage (Selected and New Poems), 2012*

Into the Deep

~~ William Scott Galasso – ©2012 ~~

Open your heart, see
with your hands there are rivers
and streams beneath this skin,
free the adhesions and hear
them sing. Note rolling hills of muscle
balled like clenched fists feel them
move under your palms. What does
this body say when it speaks, what
secrets lie buried in tissue? Pain
crouches deep and fears exposure,
but the heart wants closure and its
freedom at last. Let your hands
give wings to that heart. Let the light
of heaven and the energy of earth
flow through you. Channel it, help
the body cleanse the spirits house
with its healing gift. Be here now, let
the dreamer, reclaim the dream.

Credit: *Collage (Selected and New Poems), 2012*

Blue Skies Girl

~~ William Scott Galasso – ©2013 ~~

Blue skies girl
do you carry yet
a memory of me
as I still do, so many
years later of you

Maple

~~ William Scott Galasso – ©2013 ~~

Root to branch, bud to leaf,
tree hydraulics lifting up
from winter sleep, deep
water from rich earth
and the sustenance of sun.
Yellow/green in spring,
unfurling like flags under
robin's egg skies. Veined
like rivers, triolets, wide
and spatulate, giving shade
and a sonorous sound to
nesting birds, cyclists, those
fortunate enough to picnic
beneath them.

In summer days enduring
long, searing heat, the kind
that on city street melts tar
in its white hot glare, until
after lightning, after rain,
one day the coolness lingers.

And the maple in its hues
mimics sunset as we enjoy
the glucose gift of sap, rich
blood before the first snow
now imminent and the leaves
become dry as our skin does,
becomes parchment, then mulch
as our bones do and we share
their fate to earth returning.

Roulette

~~ William Scott Galasso – ©2012 ~~

I know what hat she wears
in the garden on a summer's day,
how she savors a mango margarita
and her favorite cranberry scarf.

I know the music that makes
her dance and which words
quiver like hummingbird wings,
when she fears to say too much.

And I've learned to translate
the language of her eyes,
can predict in them clear skies,
bad weather or a secret long
hidden, soon to be born.

and I'm attuned to the sharps
and flats of her voice, can
tell when we harmonize or
conversely are bent by discord
or *something* left unsaid.

and I know her safe's combination,
the ministrations that curl her toes
and the place she calls comfort
when she rests her head on my chest.

No alchemy this, call the magic
due diligence; achieved by learning
when to listen, when to speak,
when to laugh... and when to
simply hold her.

Credit: Collage (Selected and New Poems), 2012

Daylight

~~ Amanda Rachelle Geers – ©2013 ~~

It is simple
to love me
            when you
find me a stone,
smooth and flat,
that soothes my touch.

I know the waves
washed and dremeled
the brittle away
and you knew it too.

It is this:
simply love me.
            Would you
hold my chest?
I'll hold your head,
and hold what passes between.

How the moon cradled the sun-
she said, there is a time to sleep
and he kept warm in the dark side,
when he rose, she rose too.

Our love is simple:
daylight moon.

Inspired by a *Birds & Blooms* Q&A Article
~~ *Amanda Rachelle Geers – ©2013* ~~

inches long.

up each spring and
broken foliage,
   but they've never
like beautiful purple.

What can I do to coax them?

inching along,

shade and overcrowding
common culprits when done
   if you aren't
in full.

irises
under the half bloom.

Pancha Rathas
~~ Amanda Rachelle Geers – ©2013 ~~

a monument complex in Mahabalipurnam,
an example of Indian monolithic rock-cut architecture

A goat kid sleeps on a dancing statue:
turquoise worn and paused in-step,
one foot raised and waiting
to feel the slap against the stone.
It seems all hang on that final
beat, even the monolith temples
wait for their builders' return,
when they'll bow against the
sanded floors in narrow openings
between corridors.

And outside the city wait the cross-
legged guards , crazed and cloudy-eyed,
as vacant and indifferent as the sun
gathering in the pavement and beating
through their bones. But for their disfigured hands;
alive enough to open to the movement
in passing crowds of silhouettes and footsteps,
and hang in the air for the drop of a coin--
for the turn of its fated faces.

Wish You Were Here

~~ Amanda Rachelle Geers – ©2013 ~~

I was wondering if you remember when we floated
down the Boise River? How we were the only ones.
All the rest had left, gone back to school;
but we stayed floating, spinning in shaded rapids
and whirlpools. The tire rubber burned the back
of my thighs, the parking lot gravel was too hot for your feet.
At two, we boarded the bus home, and sat in the back
near the emergency exit, confronting Death.
We told him he had invaded your dad's personal space
and asked him to stay away from us all for a while.

Or how that same evening we drove up to the cliff
that overlooks the city. A desert fox
had stalked us, following the brake lights.
We stood against the passenger doors, and I told
you how I've always been lonely, always,
as the neon cross peered over the cliff with us.
I'm wondering now if you remember when you told me
how you could never let another tear us apart?
We should have stayed there:
wind-chapped and standing on heights.

We aren't in the glacier river anymore, not scrambling
down cliffs toward the bank. We aren't on the side
of the road with the hood popped open,
our drinking water splattered to cool the engine.
We aren't laughing anymore at the driver
who nearly ran us off the road. You're in bible school now,
and I hope everything's going well . . . reading the Scriptures.
But I am on the cliff still, with the wild fox, and the light
from the cross offends my eyes as I peer into the dark gulley
between this cliff and you somewhere near the river below.

The Corner Tree

A Triolet

~~ *Amanda Rachelle Geers – ©2013* ~~

I think God's waiting for me down in the corner tree
where the robins and chickadees gather in the rain;
full and singing wet, bare in what they foresee.
I think God's waiting for me down in the corner tree:
the one I pass on my returns, the one cluttered with debris.
Silent, and still. His outstretched limbs remain.
I think God's waiting for me down in the corner tree
where the robins and chickadees gather in the rain.

Be Careful, Young Woman

~~ Donald R. Green – ©1996 ~~

He promised to give her all of his love
Forever, complete, and inspired from above,
To give her all of the stuff of life
If only she'd agree to become his wife.

She married him and gave him her strength,
Cooking and cleaning, chores at great length.
For eighteen years she often denied
Her own needs to serve him and support his pride.
For all of this time she was an excellent wife,
Who stayed with him through unemployment and strife.
She helped and encouraged, and comforted him
Especially when the money ran dreadfully slim.
She called on her parents to help him along
By giving him money when things went wrong.
Her slender beauty, her calmness and wit
Were gifts she bestowed on him (as he'll admit).
She gave birth to three children, all of them his
But as the years rolled by it all came to this:
He was a child in man's clothing, variable and weak,
Forgetting his promises and beginning to seek
more pleasure and excitement than he could find in a wife,
Causing her much misery, suffering and strife.
He got a good job, a good turn in his life
Inherited a fortune (no need for a wife).

He thought he could find love in the arms of another,
But really was seeking to find his own mother.
He divorced his wife of so many years
And caused her to soak her pillow with tears.

She had to return to her earlier profession,
(She'd learned computers in an earlier school session).
Thank God for her intelligence that was so abundant,
That she found high pay in work not redundant.

Years from now, when he's old and gray,
Her ex 'll look back o'er his life and say:
My God what happened, what've I done
For temporary pleasures I thought would be fun.
I gave up a good woman who loved me more years,
Than I've spent with other women that ended in tears.
Too bad, old man, it's completely too late
To go back to that wife of the earliest date.

Now, young girl, here's a lesson to be learned:
Don't marry a man until he has earned
The right to be called a man worth his salt
Who can bear the strain of real life's assault.
Get yourself educated in salable skills
Before you get married and head for the hills.
For life is never as easy and smooth
As a young man's offerings when making his move.

Staying married for life takes a lot more than talking.
It takes patience, and kindness and freedom from sulking.
A hurried mistake in choosing a mate
Can cause a lifetime of misery and spate.
Take time, and be careful young woman in choosing,
So you won't join the ranks of the ones who're loosing!

Ruby

~~ Donald R. Green – ©2011 ~~

A crocheted bunny sat outside her door,
Waiting for the one who'd return no more.
For death came to visit her one night,
Taking her forever from our sight.
And the little rabbit sat gathering dust,
As a thing uncared for always must.
The hands that cared for it forever gone,
To the light eternal, on and on.

But, then one day the rabbit wasn't there,
Picked up by a loving friend or heir
Perhaps now, the bunny's found a home
And is again a symbol of love and shalom

Cow Docs

~~ Del Gustafson – ©2013 ~~

The day is hot the dust is deep,
the calves are all well grown,
Big. strong and range bred wild,
it's hard to get them thrown.

Wild eyed at the ropes end,
Bucking and bawling in fright,
Until one snorts and shakes his head,
And then goes on the fight.

Tail raised, he drops his head,
Charging right at the crew,
The cowboys running for the fence,
As the steer comes busting through.

A cowboy tangled in the rope,
Had better try to get unwound.
Before the steer charges off,
Dragging him across the ground.

If a cowboy can't beat him to the fence?
The one thing that you can trust,
The Steer will knock that cowboy flat.
And roll him in the dust.

Rope burns, bruises, busted ribs,
Painful stomped on feet,
The cowboys may need more doctoring,
Then the stock they meant to treat.

Dust

~~ Del Gustafson – ©2013 ~~

I cough and wheeze, gasp and then sneeze,
From the cloud blown by the last gust.
Slapping a rope to the rear of a slow moving steer,
As we move in that billowing dust.

Dust from my hat to boot toes, dust up my nose,
A powder the color of rust.
Those thin boney steers from their tails to their ears,
Look alike in their coating of Dust.

The wind blows it around till it falls to the ground,
Where it settles to a hard barren crust,
We need rain I know to make the grass grow,
But all we get is more dust.

We couldn't plant cotton or grain for lack of rain,
Another year and I think I'll go bust.
We sold the tractors and plows to buy feed for the cows,
They couldn't survive on just dust.

My loan payments are due and my taxes are too,
And I feel it is really unjust,
What we produce on this land has no demand,
There just is no market for dust.

The Preacher said friend it will come to an end,
Stay strong in your faith and your trust,
But I'm afraid when I die it will still be bone dry,
And I'll return as just more blowing dust.

Honest Herb

~~ Del Gustafson – ©2013 ~~

I met up with Herb the other day as he came riding down the trail,
He had a young pinto mustang tied to his horse's tail,
I gave her a good look over, Herb never said a word,
But I suspected he had roped her from a mountain mustang herd.

I said, Herb, The thing about your horse chasing I never understood,
You go to church most Sundays and folks say you are good,
But I'm thinking about that Paint filly tied to your horse's tail,
If the BLM caught you with her you'd be fined or go to jail.

I know you think the government is run by crooks and fools,
We caught horses there for years before they changed the rules,
They round them up and ship them off, they spoiled all our fun,
But they will arrest a man for stealing if they catch him taking one.

Herb replied, you know I am a Deacon and that my faith is strong,
And I have always been a true friend and will never do you wrong,
Another man's cash or a branded calf, you know I'd never take it,
And any law that I agree with, there's no way I'd ever break it.

But the property tax and grazing fees are really getting high,
And with feed and groceries going up we are barely getting by,
And federal and state income tax on every dime I earn,
So I try to catch a horse or two as a little tax return.

I looked that filly over and scratched my head in thought,
She sure had better breeding than the last horse that I bought,
The government might call it stealing and claim that it is wrong,
But next time Herb goes chasing mustangs, I'm gonna tag along.

The Stranger

~~ Del Gustafson – ©2013 ~~

He rode up to the cabin,
The air was cold and still,
His ragged Mackinaw was old,
And did not keep out the chill.

The barn collapsed years ago,
A pile without form,
He blanketed his horse with his slicker,
Trying to keep him warm.

His ride had been bitter cold,
As through the drifts he strove,
He had coal oil for the oil lamps,
And wood to feed the stove.

He had not crossed this threshold,
In fifty years or more,
He felt a wave of deep remorse,
As he stepped through the door.

He laid a fire in the stove,
And got it burning bright,
Filled the lamps and trimmed the wicks,
To fill the room with light.

He brewed a pot of coffee,
In Ma's enamelware pot,
And spread a simple Christmas meal,
From the few things he had brought.

As he sat and sipped his coffee,
In his mind he could still see,

The meals his mother served there,
The decorations on the tree.

This cabin he had once called home,
A refuge filled with joy,
With Ma and Pa and sisters,
He was the only boy.

He wiped the family pictures,
That were still hanging there,
And took his seat near the stove,
In the remains of Pa's old chair.

This home was once filled with love,
Joy and Christmas trees,
The crackling fire made him recall,
Those long gone memories.

The sound of Pa's loud laughter,
Ma's giggles and her smile,
Soft whispers of his sisters,
Lived again for a short while.

He'd ridden out on his own trail,
And the years had rolled on past,
His loved ones now were dead and gone,
He was the very last.

This will be his last ride,
His pilgrimage now was done,
He'll ride out, not to return,
With the rising of the sun.

Wild Herds

~~ Del Gustafson – ©2013 ~~

The prairie stretches far as can be seen,
Under a deep blue sky
Cloud chimneys ride the upper winds,
Giant white pillars drifting by.

The golden grass heads bow as one,
Bent by the constant breeze.
Prairie flowers with purple blooms,
Rise above my horse's knees.

The cattle move slow in the summer heat,
With head and horns hanging low.
They want to lie down to chew their cud,
And with reluctance plod on slow.

Then distantly the drumming of hooves,
Faint at first but very clear,
The hoof beats grow louder still,
galloping, galloping, coming near.

Wild horses stream over the grassy plain,
Breathtakingly beautiful in their flight,
All colors of duns, sorrels, bays and roans
Piebald steeds of brown and white.

The magnificent herd passed and disappeared,
Running, running, on and on.
The prairie surrendered to the farmers plow,
And the wild herds were gone

At the Cemetery
~~ Nan Harty – ©2013 ~~

I do not imagine the dead must be overjoyed
when mourners in black dresses and black suits
white tissues and white handkerchiefs,
balls of salt and grief in their fists, walk
arm in arm, shoulder to shoulder to depart
toward the cavalcade of cars that brought them.

I do not imagine the dead must be overjoyed
as strangers step in close to lower them down
to rest amid the rows of others gone before;
as dirt tossed on top of them rattles the quiet,
a fresh mound is tamped and rounded,
sweet flowers left on top; the funeral canopy
removed and even the grave keepers depart .

I do not imagine the dead must be overjoyed when
the curtain finally torn in half closes on this life
and opens upon the next step. The living and the dead
each left to go on one without the other
wary of the epilogue to come.

Answers for Pablo Neruda

~~ Nan Harty – ©2013 ~~

There are no churches in heaven.
A tree's roots are its brains.
Volcanoes never get ulcers.
A cat has no questions, only answers.
Oranges share well.
Rubies and juice of pomegranate are first cousins.
Suspenders retired long before vests voted to revolt.
There are ten translators of the language of whales in the world.
The earth has been lent for a brief time to the sea, not visa versa.
Some hate the country smelling of manure and sun.
Birds volunteer to lead the way when a flock takes flight.
The child you were is not gone.
The tallest trees translate the earth to the sky.
Solitary sheep choose to take a break from the group.
It is where I was lost that I finally found myself.
Old people do remember their debts and burn with desire,
at least old poets do.

On The Edge
~~ Nan Harty – ©2013 ~~

Despite her efforts,
the seventy something hostess with twenty something
shoulder length hair, curled, tastefully bottle browned,
not a trace of gray;
her figure still thin but no longer lithe,
tastefully bejeweled hands and throat,
voguish black outfit, scooped neckline,
looked every bit her age, for she was exhausted
four hours into an eight hour morning shift,
forty plus years into restaurant work,
thousands and thousands of hours on her feet,
years from the dream of opening her own restaurant,
a lifetime away from bussing tables for her father and mother.
Like so many of us she is on the edge, the demarcation line,
not between youth and middle age,
rather the boundary line between middle age and old age.
Given her apparent efforts,
this time of her life must seem like a ledge,
an abyss below and beyond,
bounty and beauty behind her.

I Never Grow Tired of the Country
~~ Nan Harty – ©2013 ~~

I never grow tired of the country,
how a country day holds the silence,
how evergreens stand tall like cathedral spires,
how a pond gets set with a flock of geese.
I have been thinking about the country's spirit,
how a deer catches our breath,
how a farm fence keeps in more than keeps it out,
how clothes hung on the line on a warm summer day
smell fresh the same way for mother after mother after mother.
How the moon rises and it seems to wander across a dark sky.
How, if otter or heron visit and rest on the dock,
it's as if someone famous comes unannounced.
How a seat in a chair in this yard, with this view,
on any given day is a church pew, a prayer mat.

A Chair in the Sun
~~ Nan Harty – ©2013 ~~

Inspired by *A Chair in the Snow* by Jane Hirshfield

A chair in the sun, whether Adirondack
wooden or plastic,
meshed or metal, old rusty blue or neon green

is a chair in the sun which is always a welcome
more than a smile
more than a handshake or a hug -
a sunny chair is there for just one thing
to bask a body in a moment and a place
while
planes move through overhead blue
full of others going, going, gone.

Cat Shelter

~~ David D. Horowitz – ©2013 ~~

Oak planks extend from walls. On floor, eight hampers
With door and air holes service feline campers
Curled up inside on checkered flannel pads.
Cats snooze as lamplit traffic cruises past
The plate-glass windows guarding them. Twilight--
Half-tabby--licks her forepaws clean. Stylite--
Half-Persian, mellow as a meatloaf--rests
With paws and tail infolded, purrs and nests.
Augustine, Swami, Sprint munch tuna, lap
Fresh water, stretch a bit and start to nap,
As Twilight calms her grooming, meditates
On traffic, lamplight, moon, and gutter grates.
I pass the windows, grin, not tapping glass,
Admiring their quietude; the gloss
Of creamy, sable, cloudy fur; suave cool.
Their room's penumbra glints a golden jewel
For every open eye, and Twilight sniffs the night
For danger, finding none. I breathe, stare, not
Budging. For here's contentment, peace, and calm,
As much as could be heard in any psalm.
Tomorrow they might yowl and scamper,
Dispute two inches in a hamper:
Who knows? But now, no whimper. Calm pervades
My blood. Their silence slows me. Night provides
These cats' example. Yes, I'd rather nestle
Into a comfy bed tonight than wrestle
With more detail. I'd rather purr than hiss.
I'll sharpen claws tomorrow. Now I'll kiss
And hug, connect and meditate in silence
And leave the world its haste and violence.

Extension

~~ David D. Horowitz – ©2013 ~~

Hand separates to fingers, fringe,
And forearm leads to elbow's hinge.
There's beefy bicep bulging strength
And shoulders sloping into length.

My hand: a tool to help me reach,
Snare, tie, connect, release, free, read,
Compose. My fingers fringe my hand
And join yours, bridging island, land.

Place for Pages
~~ David D. Horowitz – ©2012 ~~

You'd browse, then buy a bargain paperback.
Now *CLOSED*, front window smashed to spider web of crack,
Used bookstore morphs into graffiti canvass
For those adjacent to the pricey campus.
I'm thrilled a soup-and-sandwich shop arrives
There soon, won't mirror nearby joints and dives.
I miss the books, though, and "Beret," the tabby
Who strolled the aisles. What's to be's to be.

What better salad, though, than bookstore's discount rack?

Credit: *Sky Above the Temple,* Rose Alley Press, Seattle

To Guess and Gripe

~~ David D. Horowitz – ©2013 ~~

I guess, I glimpse, I wonder,
Can see I'm prone to blunder
And flub. God's God. I'm human.
Let creeds proclaim The New Man:
I burp, crave, gripe, and stumble,
Resent and gossip, grumble
And fumble. And I learn, pause
With patience for another's flaws.

Water of the Tigris

~~ David D. Horowitz – ©2013 ~~

A bomb in Baghdad booms, then flames and chars
Apartment fronts and blocks of dented cars,
Explodes wood crates of dates and figs, clay olive jars,
And silver trays of market's baklava and burek.
Black smoke still smolders from an ancient Buick.
A face-down corpse still clutches loaf of bread.
The muddy Tigris flows a drop more red.
Near mosque, a mother weeps at wall, at stars.

Brother

~~ Jane Boren Kaake – ©2005 ~~

Rocked alike in our mother's womb
we heard the same genetic allocations.

The chambers of our hearts echoed
with the same beating undulations.

The blood flowing warmly in our veins
issued from the same fountainhead.

The ivory elements that shaped our bones
were provided both of us, unaltered.

The very atoms of our bodies know each other,
recognize a kinship that will never sever—

Or know their sweet eternal brotherhood.
Will I not know my brother forever?

The Beauty Shoppe
~~ Jane Boren Kaake – ©2002 ~~

In the paneled halls of
the temple of extravagance,
marbled floors deny
the dents of spikey heels.
Twig-thin handmaids, black clad,
scurry, carry sacred instruments
of ritualistic artifice
to serve the vestal faces—
mirrored, expectant, and hopeful.

Shelves hold small bottles of color,
and pots of subtle tints—
sheens of pearl and apricot,
pencils and brushes
and manufactured sponges.
The air reeks with perfumes—
sensual fragrances of sybaritic oils,
hairspray is a misty smog.

Background music permeates—
the hallowed halls, in decibels
that excite the murmuring flock.
The rocky, unremitting rhythm
challenged by exclamatory chings
of cash registers.

Eyes dazed with surfeit of indulgence,
young girls emerge from the glass doors,
their faces blanched porcelain,
sketched brows arched to parentheses,
and painted lips of brilliant hues.
Tender, slender necks support

Nefertiti heads with piles of curls—
and tortured squiggles hanging
like a sweating peasant's hair.
It's Prom Night.

The Geography of the Universe
~~ Jane Boren Kaake – ©2002 ~~

In the vast and limitless universe
and in the infinity of unfettered eons—
loom roiling masses of luminescence,
gravid with embryonic stars.

Within that vaulting, celestial sweep,
smokey with star dust, a galaxy wheels—
spiraling its trailing arms, swirling
with clusters of radiant bodies—

Among those nameless, shining billions,
pulsates a unique and glimmering star.
In perfect balance of light and heat,
it nurtures a wondrous planet.

Soaring in an ordained orbit, Earth spins.
Sister planets move close, move off,
in ordered, unalterable configurations—
a ponderous planet minuet.

Imprisoned y gravity, Earth's creation,
Man, stands gazing out to the immensity.
Awestruck and beset with longing,
he yearns to soar among the stars.

March of the Warriors
~~ Jane Boren Kaake – ©2005 ~~

The power of a thousand feet marching
reverberates across America's lands.
Star spangled banners unfurl, wind rippled;
trumpets flash, cymbals clash in brass-filled bands.

Young warriors in cherished uniforms –
faces solemn with selfless dedication –
tromp straight-backed in military quick-step –
steely eyed with determination.

Proudly, stalwart remnants of other wars –
old eyes shining with remembered glory,
chests agleam with merited honor bars,
slow march to their place in history.

Watching this parade, throngs of relatives
and patriotic folks in dazzled admiration,
applaud, with swelling pride-filled hearts,
these brave warriors of a grateful nation.

When at last the music and the speeching's done,
and left behind the fallen heroes' graves'
honor fusillades and hear-searing-Taps
will speak honor to American braves.

Who *Really* Goes There?

~~ *Jane Boren Kaake – ©2008* ~~

Who goes there on the world stage?
Who are those now seeking power?
Are high of wisdom and intellect?
Or are they just attractions of the hour?

Are they only poseurs seeking office?
Do they own true superiority?
When they speak with "sincerity,"
do they merely seek popularity?

Amidst balloons and confetti—
the hullabaloo and screaming shouts,
are we dazzled and mesmerized
until our judgement brains run out?

Their presentations are ingenious,
with honeyed words and toothy smiles aglare.
What's behind their magicians' tongues?
Will we ever truly know, who goes there?

Across America they run like rats,
exhorting, cajoling. They aver,
each one, to make the changes that we need,
so that we'll have the bet world ever.

The stakes are high so truth is bent,
and slanders race across the land.
What choice have we who agonize?
How can we make an informed stand?

Open Crown

~~ Lynn Kopelke – ©2013 ~~

Each day starts out like a brand new hat
With an unshaped open crown
But in the course of events it don't stay like that
Subject to life's ups and downs.

Pretty soon there's a pinch here and a bash there.
Some days it looks like it's been hit by a truck.
So you punch it out 'til it looks middlin' fair
And remind yourself to remember next time to duck.

But some dents just won't punch out.
So you learn to live with the scars.
And you come to figure that's what its all about.
The good and the bad make up what you are.

Pretty soon that old hat suits you to a tee
Showin' off your own peculiar style.
The secret to weatherin' life's dinks and dings 'tween you and me
Always keep your brim in the shape of a smile!

Beauty's Work
~~ Herbert C. McClees – ©2012 ~~

Beauty glimpsed in fabric, drape and form;
In cutting, stitching, sewing expressed;
For a moment, can be touched,
when worn,
In the admiration of her dress.

Some would hold Beauty cheap
and sell her dear
As the latest fashion, haute couture,
for a diva (to Beauty a stranger, though near);
A prop for her drama, a lure.

But for many, Beauty is sweated
in fittings and alterations,
Is present in a sewing machine's ticking
while children, nearby play;
Is felt in a mother's devotion
and a daughter's adoration;
And lived in her labor, oblivious
to the tick-tock of fashionista stilettos.

*In Laura King's art sewing machine stitches
are used to outline fashion design sketches.*

*"To be born woman is to know –
although they do not talk of it at school –
that we must labour to be beautiful."
–from "Adam's Curse" by W. B. Yeats,*

The Scarf

~~ Herbert C. McClees – ©2013 ~~

She visits him once a year in the Fall
When the raking is nearly done,
To catch-up and pass the time.

Far off, in the chilly dawn,
Birds trill as she speaks;
Standing or kneeling (there is no bench);
She brings news of the family, the kids;
and her garden;

Pausing from time to time,
(clipping here and there);
She finds more to say,
In response, perhaps,
to a quiet question or a memory's tug.

As the sun clears the distant trees,
She lays her own work aside,
a scarf of remembrance:
Made from the threads of their lives;
Knit with words remembered and said
from dawn visits over the years,

A warming scarf against the coming winter;
And now, having mended its snags and pulls –
she can wait and dream.

Before long, catching the morning light,
A bright red and orange maple leaf,
Cartwheels into view to rest
Near a small flag which
unfurls and furls;

And then, she feels her hair
being gently stroked;
As their days, months, and years,
together and apart,
Rank on rank, pass in review,
In honor of Life's veterans.

Scenes in the Park
~~ Herbert C. McClees – ©2007 ~~

A man sprinting,
Towards children leaping,
In bronze;
Followed by a little girl,
Who toddles off –
To a bed of flowers.

Sitting on a bench,
A little boy to his dad:
"A great way to watch football!"
His reply: "No, it's baseball."

At the beach waiting:
Three little girls in swim suits,
While a man inflates a small boat,
On his knees.

Debutante Ball

~~ Herbert C. McClees – ©2007 ~~

A rambunctious cotillion
Of dubious belles,
Rung too soon or too late,
Encircles and dissipates
In colorful clutter and flimsy pretense.

After the debutants' presentation,
Stirring music (and a drink or two)
Effects a magical transformation
From gala ball to naval review.

The dancing throng becomes an ensign fleet
Maneuvering before an admiral's flotilla
Anchored in the bay!

Each maiden ship is under the gallánt command
of a junior officer,
Who must tack his new vessel, hands on,
And issue crisp orders,
(not always obeyed, and sometimes unheard)
Over the martial music of the escadrille
Playing for a crenellated line.

In the spectator fleet, retired captains and wives,
Hold their spy glasses high;
And study their bonny ship's quick turns,
Braced with a tonic of pride and anxiety.

Some ships' courses are sailed with grace
While others are cut perilously close,
Requiring a hard turn to port,

Or suffering, a bump amidships (or worse,
torn rigging or sails)!

As the spectacle ends, the vessels are returned
By lieutenants eager for a new command;
Save for a one buccaneer heart,
Who heads out to sea
Sailing his first prize
And captured crew!

Shopping Cart Cowboy

~~ Herbert C. McClees – ©2012 ~~

1

We round up carts and head 'em out,
on endless asphalt plains;
And drive 'em to market,
in a clatter of wobbly wheels.

(Chorus)
I'm a shopping cart cowboy
on another roundup drive;
We herd 'em to the feed lots,
where, they're stuffed to bust their sides.

Yippy yi yea, yippy yi yo;
Punchin' steel to stay alive!

2

Though feed lot rustlers nab 'em,
we bring every dogie home;
And most times, steel ribs showing,
I must trail 'em back, alone.

(Chorus)

3

After bedding down my herd,
I sing lonesome to the stars
When dogs howl or sirens wail,
I double with my guitar.

(Chorus)

A shopping cart cowboy!

Tune: "Ghost Riders in the Sky"

Flight to Arcata *(Angie's Voice)*

~~ Denise Calvetti Michaels – ©2010 ~~

The girl who will become my mother is dropped off at the curb.
At seventeen she will not remember the hug or the words
before her mother drives away, leaving her at the airport.

I want to warn the girl she'll be haunted by the knot
that binds the past to the future, invisible like the fold
of the gull's wing as the plane lifts, flocks of birds falling away.

Today she's chosen the seat next to the window; a teenager
with the helter-skelter cowlick of bangs she can't subdue, white
frost lipstick Aunt Winnie told her never to wear.

First in her family to go to college, my mother answered phones
to earn tuition. But what if she had been turned away?
Not experienced the liberation as the plane lifts; liberation

the word she wouldn't have spoken or used in a sentence
—I liberate myself, I chose liberation, the phrase to mean hope
in the midst of flight; there'll be something more for those who run
away.

On a hiking trip, as we gather kindling for the fire,
my mother will tell me the felt thing is true
like the green twig's arc.

If poetry is her calling, it's how the pen takes its place in her
hand, what the blank page means—table, window, refuge and the
    wall
to rebel against, inseparable.

The girl who will become my mother clutches the journal
to herself on the plane.

I want to tell her she'll be haunted by sensations of departure,
the knot the place the past became dislocated, disruption the sound
of birds she thought had no song.

Credit: *Jack Straw Writers Program, 2010 & City Works Press, 2011*

In the Cascade Mountains Late in the Year

~~ Denise Calvetti Michaels – ©2004 ~~

Descending softly over Icicle Creek, snow lingers,
a descant, in the still of cold mountain air.

Outside the cabin window, pale limbs of yearling birch
recall the early poems of Robert Frost
when earth was a pear-green place,
choice, common as seed.

Perhaps it's that I'm alone, reading
in the *New York Times*
Pavarotti's remarried, has a new daughter,
a one-year old named Alice, left behind his first wife
and their three daughters in Padua.

Perhaps it's that my mother-in-law is slipping away,
a frail moon who won't eat,
while the shadow of my father lengthens
over California, touches the map where I was a child.

Or maybe it's the way the cabin's cedar siding is stained
by the charcoal rime of winter's jagged line,
deepening this song, a B-flat minor melody,
strummed long ago, on a wayfarer's guitar.

There, I, too, belong, with the tribe at the circle fire,
interludes of snow falling,
a descant in the still of cold mountain air.

Credit: *Wetlands Review, 2004 & WPA, Mute Note Earthward, 2005*

My Dearest Sister,

~~ Denise Calvetti Michaels – ©2012 ~~

Today is clear and cold, and a week since I
thought I'd lose the baby. Please don't worry—
the midwife says everything will be fine. This
past winter I thought I'd lose my mind though
everyone warned me—cabin fever, long dark
days, rains that flood here in early November.
By now, Sis, I've slept through my first rainy
season—toppled trees, storm-tossed branches
flung to the roof; resinous rain woven into the
warp and weft of my nightmares and dreams,
the wind's howl the first lullaby the little one will
hear. Sometimes, middle of the night, to escape
four walls, Darius gone a month on the Sauk
felling cedar stumps for shingle bolts, I open
the cabin door and stand on the threshold to
welcome the deluge, our little plat like the muddy
Missouri when we were girls, wading knee-deep,
across the ditch, to fetch eggs in the barn—I
held your hand, Pa made us the oak plank he
swore would last forever. Writing to you helps,
some things I didn't realize—road of our town all
boulder and mud, clots of mud alongside wagon
ruts, one tree, dear to us, the townspeople let
stand between Eagle's Tavern and the Redmond
bank—I'm grateful, a newcomer, trying to make
a home, follow the path leading off the frame—
Sister, no photograph is ever vast enough to
capture a life—the hope I felt this morning when
I came out of the dark woods into the clear-
cut, the baby kicking, four girls dressed in their
Sunday best standing in the muck like crocuses.

Credit: *Redmond Centennial Poems, 2012*

After the Robin Hit the Window You Call

~~ *Denise Calvetti Michaels – ©2006* ~~

Tilted head lolling tawny feathers,
toothpick legs crazed as old porcelain,
the oval of her body limp in the realm

of your palm and cupped, like holy water,
elusive as mercury, and the lyric
moment, a story you confide in me of boyhood,

its tropical location, a dozen doves
spelling *harmony* in shale at the edge
of wisteria, veranda doors open,

your mother playing the grand piano
where I can see you, age four, listen
to broken-chord arpeggios

before the keys sting her fingers
and you soothe her,
before the river turns to canteen-tin

at the bend of the Adam's apple
and your father blurs in a thicket of jays
as you climb the sill to become the boy

in Miami birds turn to, trusting the pieces
of bread in your hand
—and cell phone to cell phone we talk

you on your way to work, me already there,
only our cells to hold the stillness, to lift her.

Credit: *Crosscurrents, 2006*

Grandmother on the Paso Robles Ranch
Year My Father Was Born

~~ Denise Calvetti Michaels – ©2006 ~~

Agostina Gonella Bianco.
Born 1887, Montaldo Scarumpi, Italy. 1982, Redwood City, California

Looking back, women chat under oak shade,
crochet stars into blankets, blankets into stars.

Stiff as quills, cattails border the walk.
Crow hops away on one foot, tremble-light,
tawny glitter of buff weed birds.

Sun, a matchstick ember, streaks charcoal-gray sky
bronze, copper, dun—colors that glint the palette of arid places.

Hazel wrens sing in the boxwood, ranch hands smell of cow's milk.
Primipara, Agostina lingers, rapt, at the porch rail, settling in

to the good cinema in which she stars, the baby
asleep in the whir of dragonflies, temperature

one hundred degrees Fahrenheit and adobe disappears
like a riverbed mirage, abandons crickets, the neutral hues of
chameleon.

At twilight the infant's eyes focus and follow his fists
across the midline. Walls burn umber

and the house reappears from its distance with Agostina's reasons
to stay—biscuits-to-bake, oats-to-soak, polenta-to-simmer.

—Winter winces by—a dairy the place water boils,
sunrise a spell in the travail of lambing;
circles of crows, hawks and vultures, finding their zenith.

She warms a bleating newborn in gunny sack near the stove.
Calves arrive—rain roils.
Creeks torrent—chartreuse grasses grow.

When I ask if anything reminds her
of her life before America,
she turns both hands palm-side-up, reveals life-lines

—gullies, really—her gesture to explain
composing the body, a canyon-river cumulous
crisscross to snag, to open, like reveries in oak shade.

Credit: *City Works Press, 2006*

A Distant Fire
~~ Keith Moul – ©2013 ~~

Not comfortable in society's give and take,
he had accepted as his first,
meaningful gift, death.

He felt uninvolved in the coming to,
as though life were a deceit,
a painful accident occurring to others
on the next street,
as though his children would be
equally distant from life's fire.

He was not young for death.
Certainly he had faced it
when young and escaped
perhaps buoyant in the Pacific.
But over time every door
and window opened onto death.
A screen of death surrounded
each relationship; tolls of death
were always being exacted;
rewards as accounts of others
not freighted by death were tallied.

At some point, lonely in life,
he craved society with death.

At the latest moment
he reacted to death,
assuming the fetal position,
refusing nourishment,
abandoning intellect and empathy.

He may have thought, if only
higher authority would intervene
with still another supernatural joke.

He had been up to death
for months. The bottom hours
toward his final cremation
quieted him.

Inevitable Winter

~~ Keith Moul – ©2013 ~~

I wish to smell ancient blood. – John Berryman

The shaken fence peels and sags;
the stones channel the latest rain;
heath returns to purple life;
corruption under bushes adds to soil.

An old believer in spring, I snag
plentiful firewood scattered about
and fill the barrow for more heat,
to prepare for inevitable winter.

At rest now, I question how much war
inhabits so many minds, how killing
offers the first option, how hearts
merely pump the last drops of doomed blood.

My fence requires maintenance to keep
out the deer and new holocausts; stones
mark millennia; heath clings to the hill,
softly, like the best infielders' hands.

For true horror, I read Berryman's life.

True horror demands injustice as a right,
the right of one blood or another
to be spilled, in spilling smelled;
the right carried forth from ancients
as though to smell blood on a rose
incites believers to action;
and the knife is to be kept at ready.

Speculations on Absences
~~ Keith Moul – ©2013

I hadn't abandoned control.
As with an imperative tornado,
there is irksome damage
and pain of invasion.

Perhaps an uninvited but real guest,
arrived to share the moment,
including frustration with a bludgeon.

Glass shards gesture on the floor,
the smell of sweat--

there is a story to detect,
but apparently not of much good
as rarely good enters by force.

Perhaps an unknown intruder
has left me a crude version of reality.

My windows have been covered
and no additional complaint has been made.

The Circle of Life
~~ Jean Redmond – ©2013 ~~

Life is like a beautiful flower. A seed sprouts, a form grows
until ready to appear as a bud that blossoms as a smiling
baby ready to learn and grow until maturity. The circle
renews itself as new buds come with more smiling babies
blossoming and like the plant, one generation wilts away as
another circle sprouts to brighten the earth.

My Secret Hiding Place
~~ Jean Redmond – ©2013 ~~

I have a secret hiding place. Come with me, I'll share it with you.
We'll stroll through the meadow past the buttercups
    nodding in the breeze.
Can you smell the green grass so fresh from the morning dew?
Let's pause by this old stump and nibble on a blackberry or two.
Here is the path through the tall stately trees, careful,
    watch out for the delicate trilliums all in bloom.
Climb up on this tree trunk bench and enjoy my peaceful retreat.
But please, oh please, never reveal my secret hiding place.

If the moon came out only once a month
~~ Cathy Ross – ©2012 ~~

people would appreciate it more. They'd mark it
in their datebooks, take a walk by moonlight, notice
how their bedroom window framed its silver smile.

And if the moon came out just once a year,
it would be a holiday, with tinsel streamers
tied to lampposts, stores closing early
so no one has to work on lunar eve,
travelers rushing to get home by moon-night,
celebrations with champagne and cheese.
Folks would stay awake 'til dawn
to watch it turn transparent and slowly fade away.

And if the moon came out randomly,
the world would be on wide alert, never knowing
when it might appear, spotters scanning empty skies,
weathermen on TV giving odds – *"a 10% chance
 of moon tonight"* – and when it suddenly began to rise,
everyone would cry *"the moon is out,"* crowds
would fill the streets, jostling and pointing,
night events would be canceled,
moon-closure signs posted on the doors.

And if the moon rose but once a century,
ascending luminous and lush on a long-awaited night,
all humans on the planet would gather
in huddled, whispering groups
to stare in awe, dazzled by its brilliance,
enchanted by its spell. Years later,
they would tell their children, *"Yes, I saw it once.
Maybe you will live to see it too."*

But the moon is always with us,
an old familiar face, like the mantel clock,
      so no one pays it much attention.
Tonight
why not go outside and gaze up in wonder,
as if you'd never seen it before,
as if it were a miracle,
as if you had been waiting
all your life.

Credit: *If the moon came out only once a month, 2012*

The Visitors
~~ Cathy Ross – ©2012 ~~

When a quartet of sorrows
looms across your doorway,
do not run away or hide.
Let them in, take their coats.
Set aside the gifts they bring
for you must wait to open them.
Sink down into their pool of pain
until you cannot breathe
or see the sky.
Drown deep with them, hold on
as they surround you, mark
your lowest ebb in pencil on the wall.
Remember
where it lies.
And when you've learned to live your days
with them sitting on your sofa,
when you've grown accustomed
to their faces in your mirror,
to their silence at your table,
when you have lost hope
that they will ever leave,
one morning you will wake to find
no outlines on their beds,
no echoes in the hall.
You will stand alone
in the empty house of who you used to be,
hear
an eager rapping at your door,
the unthinkable return
of joy.

Credit: *If the moon came out only once a month,* 2012

After Winter

~~ Cathy Ross – ©2012 ~~

The Cheyenne call a year a winter,
counting by the cruelest season,
where endurance marks the time
and killing comes in every snow,
I think I understand it now:
    After winter
    I am older,
new lines etched upon my face
like the nets of jeweled ice
that crept across my windowpane
and somehow reached into my bones.
    After winter
    I am older,
part of me used up to fight
the unrelenting bitter cold,
like burning household chairs and tables
just to keep the fire alive.
    After winter
    I am older,
stripped open to my inner core
emptied of all certainty, my body
stiff and aching, numb,
no longer feeling
even pain.

When spring arrives, I count
the losses: ancient trees
uprooted whole, cracks in walls
too deep to mend. This year,
all the dahlias died.
This year,
I alone survived.

Credit: *If the moon came out only once a month*, 2012

Old Song

~~ Cathy Ross – ©2012 ~~

Thank goodness
the kids are grown and gone,
what would they think
of two old folks like us
moving the sofa, rolling up
the carpet, laughing as the moon
swims across the bay and the tide
erases footprints on the sand.

Touch me. Tell me again
why we started on this journey,
how we carried our box of dreams
through the cobbled streets,
how we scuffed misfortune
in front of us like dry leaves,
how we gathered up the pieces
of the sky each time it fell,
and how we finally came to understand
that all our triumphs
and all our sorrows
were merely scenery along the way.

Come. There's starlight
and the night is warm.
Play me that old song,
the one we've always loved
with saxophones and clarinets,

crank the volume up high
and open all the windows
so the noise wakes the neighbors,
then wrap me in your arms
and see if we still remember
how to dance.

Credit: *If the moon came out only once a month,* 2012

Amaryllis

~~ Cathy Ross – ©2012 ~~

One must be bold
    to bloom in winter.
One must ignore the odds,
    take a chance with snow
      and low light,
   thrust upward like a swimmer
      in a red bikini coming
    to the surface, rising high
       and higher still, until
    you are too top-heavy
       for your pot, your waxy stem
  provocative and insolent;
     your scarlet blossom
       flirtatious and seductive.
Your beauty fills my window frame,
    blurs raindrops into background.
I want to copy you, explode
    my own carnival colors,
      stick my tongue out
       at January, recklessly display
    what can be accomplished
     when the world
       is cold and dark.

Credit: *If the moon came out only once a month,* 2012

Metaphor

~~ Leonard D. Seader – ©2013 ~~

I chanced upon a tree one day,
while strolling though the woods.
A peculiar tree, not one but two.
Separate trunks twined close together
in mutual support.
Yet providing ample opportunity
for individual growth of branch and leaf.
Bright with promise,
adding beauty to their surroundings.

The world turned and time went by,
relentless in it's pace.
Once more I stood
before the pair.
Now bowed and battered
by age and storm.
Yet still entwined, with the strength of two.
Bravely facing what future remained.
Together to the end.

A Job

~~ Megan Sekreta – ©2013 ~~
[Courtesy of Elizabeth Sekreta]

you know
some days it is hard to believe
I do the things I do

can't imagine how I even got to this place
where I am free
where I perform what some call a job
the easiest task in my life

I sit upon the air
Five hundred feet above
and try to figure why they call this a job
an occupation

it's a love to me
a love of flying
of flying a helicopter

it starts from the moment I sit down in the cockpit
strap on my seatbelt
flip on the master switch
and turn the key

motor kicks over
rotors start to turn
the fun begins

feel the vibrations moving through your seat
up through the controls in a steady rhythmic fashion
get comfy and settle in for another days ride

moving down through the checklist
everything complete
pull in a little pitch
and slowly feel the point of ease
as the helicopter becomes light on the skids
and airborne we become

holding steady five feet over the ground
(I'm smiling already in anticipation
for I am only sitting in a chair writing)
maneuvering my way around the others
airplanes that is

"cleared for takeoff"
sounds through my headset
ease forward the cyclic
watching the ground quickly pass beneath my feet
and "poof" up into the other world I go
nothing better than this

they call it my job
and day after day
I sit in wonderment
exactly what that means
how could this be work
is the thought I think day after day
in my cockpit
wandering about

so in case you didn't know
or couldn't figure out...

Grandmother's Piano
~~ Linda Thompson – ©2013 ~~

Crooked fingers played beautiful music—
an irony of sound
that carried her past memories
of her youth to the blue silk
curtained apartment we shared
that cold Washington winter.

Her hands remembered
what she forgot in 85 years—
ivory gave way to her touch
progressing from a solid C chord
to the to the gentle minor of a D

At 18 I thought her life
was revealed in story
in frozen sepia tones.
But the music and the mahogany
brought her with me to the present

Handel, Gershwin, Hammerstein
joined us in music
as no words ever could
and I, the trespasser
shared a gentle secret

The music and the piano
came to me, its size
taking over my small house
No longer a granddaughter
my role now changed

I play—not an expert
but a witness to memory

a storyteller stumbling
through her melodies

It's after the sound
as the vibration of the strings
linger at my fingers
when I feel her whisper

Traveling Home
~~ Linda Thompson – ©2013 ~~

After the eating, at the end of the celebration,
The men depart—to view a new sabre saw or watch football.
Tribal unity compels me to stay
in the warmth of the kitchen with
the women, cleaning as they talk with their icy tongues.

I am inept—
knowing nothing of pie crusts, or
crock pots, or meat loaf.
I am drawn in by the ritual, but sit apart
perched on a stool slowly sipping delicate wine.

The conversation turns to recipes and
I long to find the men, but my journey led me here, so I stay.
I placate my sisters with jokes,
"I once burned a pan making soup—from a can!"
They take me on as their sport, a project.

I am trapped by ropes of recipes for
mashed-potato meat loaf and low-calorie chili
and quick and easy pot roast.
I want to scream, "Enough. This is a world I don't care
     to understand."

But I smile and reaching across the miles that separate us,
I accept recipes written neatly on note cards.
Later, on the back of them, I will write poems.

1943

~~ Linda Thompson – ©2013 ~~

canned meat product, biscuits, bouillon powder, chewing gum

> During World War II my father
> didn't pack the K-rations often
> bombardiers on missions over Germany
> got back by dinner, he said,
> or not at all. He laughed-- kind of.

biscuits, chocolate, powered coffee, cigarettes

> If I had to take them I picked the box
> that had the chocolate.
> Tasted like home? I offered.
> After a long pause—"Nothing tasted like home,"
> a hint of emotion, a surprise from my father.

granulated sugar, can opener, toilet paper, wooden spoon

> I do research—a writer's curse and pleasure
> The boxes were made by the Cracker Jack Company.
> So, I buy a box and
> a Hershey chocolate bar, go to the park
> find a nice bench in the sun

> feel the wax on the Cracker Jack box
> smell molasses and peanuts and taste my own youth.
> I open the wrapper of the Hershey bar
> take a big bite and hold it in my mouth
> sensation of velvet on my tongue.

> But it doesn't taste like home.

I think of those small boxes of food
the men carrying them into danger
in a war almost forgotten.
The last righteous war, my brother says.

I wondered what my father carried
in his rucksack and what luck
or fate carried him home.

A Chinese Beggar

~~ Paul Victor — March 2012 ~~

(A hapless, very poor man.)

As he was described, there was a hapless, perhaps pitiful man. He was deformed. His bowed head reflected a deep, unmistakable sense of profound shame and despair.

His outstretched hand beseeched random and infrequent giving of meager alms from one or another in the multitude of passers-by. Although present, he is unseen, and therefore non-existent. He does not know if, when, or how he will eat again.

Invisible in his anonymity, lost in plain sight: indeed, what would it be like to be him – not only lost, but unseen, and what others avoid seeing. Passers-by necessarily remind him of the depth of his abject unrelenting poverty, what he is not, and his impelling inconsequentialness.

Attributions to an all-powerful and knowing God; an artifact of a natural distribution, selection, and social physics; or, the terrible prerogative of a man in collision with the circumstances of his history and earned fate: these explanations are as unsatisfactory as they are incomplete.

The apparent nonchalance of passers-by – hidden by the anonymity of their vast numbers – hides a darkness and fear: a bargain that in the provisionality of their own lives, their fate can somehow never be – like *his*. There is realism to their lives, and giving to another takes away from one's own.

Somehow a convenient, anonymous other was to live this hapless, cruel fate.

A question to God: What is the purpose of a meaningless, shame-filled life of despair?

Perhaps God, if he can be found – or, He is especially found – residing in the energy and moment: the spontaneity of a warm gesture that reveals a hidden depth and the humanity of a forgotten, lost other.

A Poem for Laurie

~~ Paul Victor — May 2013 ~~

There is a futility in the use of words.

Attempting to define the gentlest breeze; a refuge from a beleaguering loneliness, the barren vastness, a piercing wind, and the coldest, freezing rain; the subtle fragrance of a rose; the song of a bird; or, the depth of love expressed by a kiss and life shared truly has no words.

The Truth of God, a symphony in the convergence of all that's shared and meaningful, the taste that is her finest exquisite wine, and the gentle touch of Laurie's hand is like the beauty of all roses that's beyond what words cannot hope to describe.

Laurie is my beautiful wife.

Agape for Ariana
~~ Paul Victor — June 2010 ~~

(My appreciation of Ariana, and what she means to me.)

Ariana as my daughter, and Laurie as my wife, are the loves of my life. We are a family defined by love – God's love. There is happiness, safety and a refuge from the freezing, piercing wind and the coldest rain in the warmth and comfort of a home we create and share together.

Ariana is the daughter I've always wanted. (I try to communicate this every day by words and deeds.)

She is a beloved beautiful flower, a rose and a gift from God who shows me His wonder everyday. (We celebrate God's grace as a family in prayer. I thank God for the love He's brought into my life.)

God is there when Ariana and her mother embrace one another in their deep, meaningful and shared bond from a lifetime of love.

She teaches that Faith is a statement of the totality of her spiritual-related experience, rather than a temporal concept of confidence.

Ariana gives me grace, and helps me want to be a better person.

Ariana is the reason for continuation and purpose. She is like a flower that blooms, nurtures and evolves. (When Laurie and I have transitioned in our time, our home can keep her family warm in an ongoing spirit of love. It is said that nothing lasts forever. That one has loved is forever.)

155

She is like a day of sunshine; her smile warms.

I look forward to seeing her and miss her when she's gone. A time not so long ago, feeling a sense of void, there was a need to call her and tell her I missed and loved her.

She, and her mother, remind me that genuine respect, trust – and love -- must be earned rather than given. I must be worthy.

We have learned of the realism of God -- the gift of Divine knowledge and truth to the extent that we can comprehend it -- in different ways.

She has a natural devotion to do God's work, help others and make the world a better more meaningful place.

There is a natural sense of protection without intrusion. The best gift I can give her is the ever-present support to grow and evolve autonomously into herself.

God is pervasive in all things; there's a Divine, universal and organizing energy. God is a source and way of genuine fulfillment and meaningfulness that is beyond our ability to comprehend. The Spiritual realm is substantive and enduring; the material is fleeting, evanescent and frangible. The Divine realm is realism, our temporal world a dream. There is an irony, a riddle: We often search for that in which we are immersed.

There is a resonance to profound truths.

Beulah "Bee" Victor
(12/23/24 – 12/20/08)
~~ Paul Victor — August 2009 ~~

Science teaches that there is truth and profound truth -- a truth whose opposite is also a profound truth.*

There is a paradox: The Spiritual is substantive and enduring; the material is fleeting, evanescent and frangible. The Divine realm is realism, our temporal world a dream. There is a resonance to profound truth.

At once she is exquisitely free in the mountains, near the ocean, and where there are wild animals and birds -- a special place where there is a convergence of nature and spirituality – a merging of our world and the other (Divine realm).

Her true essence is elsewhere: in the vast meadows and fields of flowers, visiting old friends who have passed in their time, and with her brother we missed so much. She is asking her mother all the unresolved questions that were revisited throughout her life.

There is no sadness or need for tears – for it never rains or gets so cold; there is no pain, and her disability was of this world.

A profound truth: Although she has passed, she is with me always.

* Wilczek, Frank (2008). *The Lightness of Being: Mass, Ether, and the Unification of Forces*. New York: Basic Books.

157

Better than A.A.A.

~~ Griffith H. Williams – ©2013 ~~

If I could fix myself as well
As that old motor car,
I'd never leave you flat, my dear
On asphalt, dirt or tar.

I'd never overheat again
Or shimmy when you turn.
I'd always go when it was time
To pack up and adjourn.

I'd stop each time you stomped on me
Without a cry or squeal.
I'd wipe your windshield up ahead
The future to reveal.

I'd heat your toes when you were cold
And never leak hot steam.
I'd light your nights and lock your doors
And take you home to dream.

But I'm too rough for that, I guess:
A fender dented guy,
But if you need a little help
You know I'd like to try!

Rodeo Horses

~~ Griffith H. Williams – ©2013 ~~

With my very first breath of fierce fresh air
(Moonlight and momma had just brought me home)
The rodeo horses broke free and ran;
Pounding hoof, shaking mane, ready to roam
And my swaddling self held safe to see.
I saw, how I saw! The horses were free!

They thundered up Murphy Road to Wright's Hill
By the town of Four Lakes, near the state line
White, black and chestnut, and maybe a paint.
The air roared through their lungs and roared through mine.
Daddy came up, said "Those mustangs are wild…"
I loved how earth greeted her newest child!

I never could stand to sit on a horse
'Cause the first I saw was a wild stampede
Leaping the fence like a gust of fresh air
To scatter and spread and serve its own need.
The first thing I saw gave my soul its shape,
The first thing I saw was a wild escape!

159

Diminishing Canary
~~ Griffith H. Williams – ©2013 ~~

The ancients lived abroad in heroic fresh air.
Their poetry was the lengthy hexameter.

Later, pollution reduced the verse length
As well as, perhaps, the average chest size.
Industrial smoke gaining strength
Allowed the pentameter to arise.

Later came even fouler air.
And shorter lines of song.
The poet's poor breath became rare
And the small ballad grew strong.

Now
the song
is almost
gone.

Milk Wood Words

~~ Griffith H. Williams – ©2013 ~~

With the first reading I see the poet
Brave before the bitter wind of his words.
"What courage" I think, "to really show it!"
His secrets rise before my eyes like birds.

With the second reading, I see my soul
Right there in the rhythmic fall of his line.
How could he have done it; capture me whole?
I know these secrets because they are mine.

On subsequent readings I recognize
The universal; all of us are there.
We each share a set of truths (and lies)
That the master caught with nonchalant care.

Of course his words describe himself, and me,
And you, and you for all eternity.

Sleeping in Our Pride

~~ Griffith H. Williams – ©2013 ~~

How I wish that we were lions
Sleeping in our pride
By a Serengeti shade tree,
Dust on every hide.

How I wish that we were lions
Languid with our claws
Blood dark on every muzzle,
Wrapped in ancient laws.

How I wish that we were lions,
Smooth flank shaggy mane,
Asleep beneath the broad daylight,
Safe within our reign!

Made in the USA
Charleston, SC
08 February 2014